D0891725

From Campus to Capitol

From Campus to Capitol

The Role of Government Relations
in Higher Education

William McMillen

The Johns Hopkins University Press
Baltimore

© 2010 The Johns Hopkins University Press
All rights reserved. Published 2010
Printed in the United States of America on acid-free paper

2 4 6 8 9 7 5 3 1

The Johns Hopkins University Press
2715 North Charles Street
Baltimore, Maryland 21218-4363
www.press.jhu.edu

Library of Congress Cataloging-in-Publication Data

McMillen, William.
From campus to capitol : the role of government relations in higher
education / William McMillen.
p. cm.
Includes bibliographical references and index.
ISBN-13: 978-0-8018-9459-6 (hardcover : alk. paper)
ISBN-10: 0-8018-9459-X (hardcover : alk. paper)
1. Higher education and state—United States. 2. Education,
Higher—Public relations—United States. I. Title.
LC173.M2 2010
379.73—dc22   2009038891

A catalog record for this book is available from the British Library.

*Special discounts are available for bulk purchases of this book.
For more information, please contact Special Sales at 410-516-6936 or
specialsales@press.jhu.edu.*

For Barbara

The essentials of university organization are clear and unmistakable,
and they have been handed down in unbroken continuity.
They have lasted more than seven hundred years—what form
of government has lasted so long?

—*from the Colver Lectures presented by Charles Homer Haskins
at Brown University in 1923; quoted in Haskins*, The Rise of the Universities
(Ithaca, N.Y.: Cornell University Press, 1963, 24).

It's not our job to report; it's our job to make an impact.

—*from a conversation with Bruce Johnson,
President, Inter-University Council, State of Ohio*

CONTENTS

With our sons, Christopher and Mark, who were ten and eight years old at the time, my wife, Barb, and I took the obligatory trip from northwest Ohio to our nation's capital. It was summer, and we first visited Barb's parents in Philadelphia and then traveled down to the Eastern Shore of Maryland, where Barb's grandmother still lived. Her grandfather, who had passed away, had been a waterman on the Chesapeake Bay, crabbing from a flat-bottom boat. Barb's uncle, who still worked the traps, showed us around his shanty while the boys inspected crabs and tortoises.

It was 1986, and Washington, D.C., was not very crowded when we arrived. I was a junior university administrator then and followed politics, but I had no interest in a career in government relations. During that trip more than twenty years ago, I did not visit any politicians. I did not know a lobbyist of any description. I knew nothing about the offices of the higher education associations in Washington. Instead, Barb and I were just taking the kids around to see the sights for the first time—sights like the Smithsonian's National Air and Space Museum and the Washington Monument.

We also went to the Capitol, the building my dictionary describes in sublime simplicity as the place where the "U.S. Congress meets in Washington." The four of us trudged up the massive front steps that face the mall. We walked in the front doors. As I remember it, the building was empty. Congress was not in session. There was no security. No one around. We gawked at the massiveness and the polished marble. Somehow, we found ourselves upstairs peering through the doors of the gallery to the House chamber. Sitting on the floor at each of the doors to the gallery were opened cardboard boxes. Inside was the *Congressional Record* for the day. There must have been twenty copies in each of the boxes, printed on newsprint-type paper. Maybe 150 pages long, the *Record* had no cover, just the title and the date at the top of the first page and then columns of text below. I pilfered one as an unusual souvenir of the trip. I'm sure I still have it somewhere in a box of old books.

I don't know if the boys remember that visit. Perhaps they remember the rockets and space capsules at the Air and Space Museum. I remember the museum as well, of course. But I remember better that thick copy of the *Congressional Record*. I did not know at the time that I would end up in government relations. I did not know that I would make routine flights to Washington. I did not know that I would be calling congressmen and congresswomen by their first names and go out to dinner with staffers and lobbyists. Nor did I dream that someday the surrounding streets would be barricaded, or that every building entrance would have metal detectors and police guards.

Washington, D.C., the capital of our nation, has become—always was, perhaps—a very complicated place. But so has my state capital. And, for that matter, so has my city hall. This book is about how to attempt to navigate these places. Who to see. How to get things done. Despite knowing all these things now, I've never been able to shake the memory and image of us, Bill and Barb, Chris and Mark, alone in that vast hallway.

ACKNOWLEDGMENTS

Thanks are due to Ashleigh McKown, my editor at the Johns Hopkins University Press, who first contacted me about the idea for this book. Her encouragement and careful editing are much appreciated.

I would also like to thank the following for their advice and support: Aaron Baker, Kendall L. Baker, Christopher A. Baldwin, Toni Blochowski, Andy Buczek, Patty Camacho, Dean Fadel, Diane Hymore, Rich Lewis, Denise Magner, Barbara Fialkowski McMillen (who also kept my computer working), Neil Reid, Margi Rolfe, Matt Schroeder, Kathy Vasquez, and Cynthia Wilbanks, as well as my government relations colleagues in Ohio, including the staff at the Inter-University Council, and the guys I play golf with on Sundays.

I thank the elected officials at all levels and their loyal staff members, with whom I have discussed many important issues. I have been enlightened by their dedication and honesty.

Some of the ideas in this book first appeared in my regular column "The Party Line" that ran during 2007, 2008, and 2009 in the "Careers" section of the *Chronicle of Higher Education*. The columns were written under the pseudonym Peter Onear.

Finally, I would like to thank Dr. Lloyd A. Jacobs, president of the University of Toledo. It is common for an author to recognize someone who has been instrumental in defining the issues and concepts presented in his or her book. Dr. Jacobs has been that person for me. More important, he is an example of what a new university president must be if a university is to move forward in the twenty-first century. Dr. Jacobs was willing to plunge into the complex world of local, state, and federal politics. He took time to do it, and he created a government relations staff that not only would advise him on these matters, but would also interface with politicians, agency heads, staff members, and the public. And political leaders and others in the greater community now seek his advice and counsel. Such strong partnerships between university, community, and government are the future of higher education.

From Campus to Capitol

The Rise of Government Relations Offices

The idea of employing a government relations officer at an institution of higher education has had no specific beginning. When I was the editor of my university's undergraduate newspaper in the late 1960s, I knew all of the school's administrators. I remember most of them today, and I am certain that none of them had the words "government relations" in their titles. Even today, forty years later, government relations officers often do things other than attending to their political duties. These other jobs typically include development and fund-raising, communications, and serving as the board of trustees' administrative secretary.

Today, government relations is a necessary senior administrative unit for academic institutions. Also termed "government affairs," "state or federal relations," "external relations," or "community involvement," government relations is now a vital function of virtually every college and university in America. How did this happen? How did higher education evolve to need a person or persons who would keep track of government actions? Or did the reverse happen? Did government change, increasing its influence on colleges and universities?

A few noteworthy events may help to explain the increasingly close relationship between government and higher education. As one might expect, they have a lot to do with money. A history buff might point to John C. Calhoun's 1817 Bonus Bill as the country's first earmark legislation. It directed that federal money be used to build roads in certain regions of the new country. (*Earmarks,* by the way, are congressionally directed funds allocated for specific projects.) Certainly Franklin Delano Roosevelt's New Deal legislation during the Great Depression was full of earmark-like appropriations. But such appropriations seldom directly affected universities. What we now call earmarks had no real impact on universities until the last half of the twentieth century.

- Public universities in the late 1960s and early 1970s went through rapid construction of new buildings to accommodate the Baby Boomers, who were now college-age students. Many of these students included young men who had opted to go to school and thus avoid, at least temporarily, being drafted into the military. This construction boom, fueled by state resources, forced universities to be more aware of how states were allocating campus construction funding. Universities had to become more proactive in advising state legislators about their construction needs, and in balancing residence hall construction with classroom and laboratory construction.

- Colleges and smaller universities recognized that federal grant money did not necessarily have to go only to the larger land-grant universities in their states, or to the well-known private research universities. Smaller schools were doing equally valid research and deserved a share of government funding. Earmarks as we know them today have their contemporary origins in the extensive highway construction funding of the 1950s and the Department of Defense funding of the Vietnam War. It became evident in the last quarter of the twentieth century that lobbying for "congressionally directed appropriations," as they were known in polite circles, was essential for a university's research budget.

- Joliet Junior College in Illinois, founded in 1901, was the first community college in America (community colleges are also sometimes called junior colleges). It took almost a hundred years for community colleges to find their political voice, but since about 1990 they have asserted it at both the local and state levels. Generally more nimble and better organized than public four-year schools, community colleges have gained a strong political presence—at least on the local level, and to a certain extent at the state level.

- Since the turn of the twenty-first century, government funding for universities has been extended to initiatives beyond traditional education, capital projects, and research. Increasingly, universities have been seen as engines of and resources for economic development. Certainly the concept of applied research has led to more university-held patents and the rise of technology-oriented start-up companies. Often local, state, and federal governments have provided universities with funding to promote job and business development. And following the terrorist attacks of September 11, more government funding has been made available for national security. University programs including health, criminal justice, and law often have been able to secure significant funding by being politically savvy. Most recently, there has been an infusion of stimulus funding into higher education, begun in early 2009, in response to the ongoing economic downturn.

Higher education presidents, under constant pressure from (or at least under the watchful eye of) trustees and faculty organizations, were not motivated to increase their administrative bureaucracies by establishing offices of government relations. But most presidents were also not particularly interested in spending more of their own precious time on such political activities. Therefore, the *existing* office that generally came to be tapped for government relations was the office that had the most to gain (or lose)—the university research office. Whether a university had only a couple of millions of dollars worth of grants (or less) or hundreds of millions of dollars (or more), some (if not most) of this funding came through government agencies. Even if most of the grant funding was competitive in nature and not subject to obvious political influence, university research administrators still possessed more knowledge of how the various levels of government functioned than did most other university administrators, including the president.

But from the beginning, problems with having research administrators attend to government relations work were evident. First, these administrators did not necessarily have much training in government and tended to focus on their narrow areas of mostly scientific funding. Though important, the growth of other government funding in construction projects, the arts, workforce development, and economic development often went unnoticed and untapped. In addition, shepherding grant applications through the government agencies' bureaucracies proved so time-consuming that research administrators could not afford to do the political schmoozing necessary to gain the favor of politicians.

The next group of university administrators tapped to be government relations officers were drawn from sections of the administration that dealt with community relations. These middle- to lower-level administrators were from various offices like communications and public relations, student affairs, fund-raising, continuing education and adult learning, and even athletics. Their common tie was their stake in maintaining positive relations with the surrounding community. Whether this community was a small town or the neighborhoods of a large city, the administrators were tasked with keeping the neighbors and the public happy. It was a small step to add the responsibility of keeping local politicians happy, as well.

But community-oriented administrators doing government relations work seldom had a state or federal presence. They were far down on the university administrative ladder and had little executive authority. Too often, senior administrators wanted only to see that the university's neighbors were quiet, and felt that the university had little to gain from engaging in local politics.

Next, former politicians tried their hands at being higher education government relations officers. Defeated, retired, or term-limited politicians offered universities practical political expertise. They were also comfortable associating with the university president in both social and business settings. And the university presidents, for their part, appreciated the politicians' general candor and political insights. Former politicians were also attracted by pay and benefit levels that were higher than what they had received as legislators, not to mention large expense accounts and almost no reporting oversight.

Unfortunately, former politicians doing government relations work seldom understood how universities functioned. Hobnobbing with the president at a football game or getting the president in to see the governor for fifteen minutes were pleasant activities. But neither event helped the researcher back on campus who was frantically trying to complete a $5 million alternative energy earmark before a congressional deadline. And by definition, politicians are partisan, and most were unable to become neutral in their political party affiliation. Former politicians becoming univer-

Attorneys

Oddly enough, given the number of attorneys who are politicians, it would seem logical that university general counsel offices would house government relations functions. Yet this is rarely the case. Besides being swamped with work, general counsel offices, especially at public institutions, work closely with their states' attorneys general and could be prohibited from lobbying on many issues. This potential conflict of interest has typically kept attorneys out of government relations offices.

---

sity government relations officers were duly noted by members of the other political party, who automatically resented the politicians' relatively cushy government relations jobs. The politicians were also monitored by key faculty members, who sometimes became angry over political ideas fervently retained by these university-paid politicians.

The final group of individuals who tackled government relations duties for universities were professional lobbyists. These people sometimes worked alone, but were usually members of larger supportive lobbying firms. Like politicians, lobbyists supplied a university president much crucial political savvy. But unlike politicians, they were more neutral in their political affiliations and they usually drew upon targeted expertise. In other words, they specialized in congressional earmarks, or state relations, or city government. And unlike politicians, they tended to stay in the background, doing their work quietly and efficiently.

Unfortunately for lobbyists doing government relations work, their reputations stank. This was unfair, since most lobbyists did their work well and were worth their higher price. But faculty and governing boards did not like the concept or expense of lobbyists. Presidents who used lobbyists were pressured to make certain that they produced tangible and ethically defensible results.

Researcher administrators. Community-relations employees. Politicians. Lobbyists. Most universities tried (and some still try) to manage government relations through at least one, if not all, of these options. As the managing of government relations grew more complex, university presidents found that they were spending more and more time *coordinating* government relations efforts, as well as spending more and more time *doing* government relations. Perhaps worse, presidents saw more and more of their resources being spent on government relations efforts. So the presidents were caught in a Catch-22 situation. If government relations functions were not in place, then bad things could happen. When earmarks were not funded, or state scholarship monies went to another school, or an adjacent neighborhood aggressively complained because the university invoked eminent domain to bulldoze homes, the university community—properly including the trustees—wondered why the president had not been aware of these political situations and their possible consequences, and why he or she had not done more to alleviate the situation.

What evolved at many institutions—especially at larger private universities and at larger public community colleges and state universities—was the development of government relations offices staffed not by outside politicians or consultants but by career university administrators. These administrators tended to have advanced or terminal degrees and a work history associated with both higher education policy and internal governance. These offices were often formed "under the radar" with small staffs, and with a budget that was part of the larger office of the president's budget.

In some instances, the head of the office carried the general and ambiguous title of "assistant to the president," or the government relations office was made part of another department with a traditionally close relationship to the president, such as communications or development. One advantage of this arrangement for the institution's president has been that the government relations officer often is on a first-name basis with the members of the institution's governing board. Trustees tended to give these administrators some leeway as they pursued the political goals of the institution.

Offices of government relations now exist on many university campuses, but they are perhaps the least understood of all the administrative offices. This book attempts to explain the duties of these offices and how the offices interact with other on-campus constituencies, such as the governing board, president, and faculty, as well as off-campus constituencies, such as county and city governments, state government, and the federal government. These relationships are complex and often difficult, but in the end the payoff to the university can be great.

Author's Note: I have chosen generally to use the term *university* when referring to all institutions of higher education in America. When necessary, I have used the term *community college* to refer to all two-year schools, including junior colleges. I have also used the term *private university* instead of *private college,* although many private institutions of higher education are still called colleges.

I have found it daunting to believe that I can make relevant and true comments about how all four-thousand-plus institutions of higher education handle government relations. I have interviewed numerous government relations officers and other university and education association administrators. Many institutions appear to manage government relations well, although the more I probed, the more often I found that institutions do not have a well-coordinated government relations strategy and/or mission. I hope this book encourages institutions and their presidents, trustees, administrators, and faculty to pay greater attention to government relations while also encouraging more young administrators and scholars to pursue careers in higher education government relations.

CHAPTER ONE

You Can Run, but You Can't Hide

University Presidents

In 1939, five Ohio public universities created an organization called the Inter-University Council (IUC), its purpose being to prevent the governor and state legislators from interfering with higher education. The IUC still exists and still has the same basic purpose, but its current goal, as stated by the organization's president, former Lieutenant Governor of Ohio Bruce Johnson, is "to facilitate the development of strong public policy support for Higher Education and to encourage collaboration among Ohio's great public universities." In politically correct words, he is saying to state government: "Don't interfere with us, but if you do, let us help and advise you."

The presidents of the fourteen public institutions of higher education in Ohio that now make up the IUC meet monthly in the state capital to discuss legislation, argue over collaboration, and eat a pretty good lunch. At those meetings, the presidents each bring one staff member—their government relations officer. They do not bring their provosts. They do not bring their finance officers or student affairs vice presidents. They do not even bring their board of trustees chairs. Instead, they bring their government relations officers.

This is perfectly logical. The IUC has fourth-floor corner offices in a building sitting directly across the intersection of High and Broad Streets from the state capitol. There is a view of the capitol's north steps, where Abraham Lincoln once spoke at a campaign rally. The current governor of Ohio uses the same desk where Lincoln once sat and supposedly wrote something or other. The point is that history is embodied in the nearly 200-year-old building that a university president can contemplatively gaze at when the conversation becomes boring. To whom does that university president trust this history, not to mention the well-being of his or her university? There are some seemingly logical choices: A distinguished university provost who was a biology professor? A sharp-eyed finance officer? A popular student affairs vice president? No, successful government relations between all levels of government and higher education demand the expertise of a *trained* government relations specialist.

Trained?

Okay, *trained* may not be quite the right word. At a typical IUC presidents' meeting these days, government relations officers have the following backgrounds: A novelist. A chemistry major. A fund-raiser. One former Republican legislator and one former Democratic legislator. A women's volleyball coach. An attorney who makes his living as a lobbyist. Two assistants to the president. The daughter of a former state legislator. The former administrative head of the Republican state senate caucus. And two current faculty members who are trying to become provosts in a future life. Not one of these persons has a degree in government relations, which is not all that unusual, seeing as how there are pretty much no degrees in government relations offered by any university anywhere.

Nevertheless, this oddly gathered collection of assorted individuals exerts great influence on their presidents and the future of their universities.

Government relations officers and their staff (if they're lucky enough to have a staff) have become the front line, facing an increasing barrage of government intervention into higher education. To be sure, this is not a one-way street. This is not all about conservative or liberal legislators demanding that certain courses be taught. It is not about a secretary of education trying to join federal student loan funding and university accreditation at the hip. Nor is it about local community agencies demanding that universities fund economic development initiatives, or about the Chinese government offering universities land to build branch campuses there.

It is about much more. On the positive side, it is also about the hundreds of millions of dollars that flow out of Washington for university research. It is about the hundreds of millions of dollars that flow out of state coffers for state subsidy. It is even about local municipalities bending over backwards to accommodate university and university foundation zoning and tax abatement requests to promote economic development.

Universities spend an awful lot of time being on the defensive politically. But just as often universities are on the offensive. Just like the original IUC purpose in 1939: Give us money and don't interfere with us. Standing at the center of this push-and-pull struggle are the university's government relations officer and the university president.

Contemporary university presidents have a problem. No one fully comprehends the parameters of their job—including the presidents themselves. University presidents are so exhausted by the years and struggles associated with assuming the office that when it finally falls to them, they have little time and less energy to contemplate what they are supposed to do. And a new president is often admonished, virtually the moment she takes office, by the board, staff, and faculty, not to be like her immediate predecessor. If the previous president was active and boisterous, the new president should be quiet and contemplative. Or, if the previous president was quiet and contemplative, the new president should be active and boisterous. If the old president had never fired anyone, the new president should clean house. Or, if the old president enjoyed firing people, the new president should stay the course with the current personnel. If the old president never traveled to raise money, the new president should get out there and start hitting up the alumni. Or, if the old president traveled all the time to raise money, the new president should stay on campus and tend to business.

You get the picture. So, what is a president supposed to do? Well, first of all, put together an accurate job description. A university president's job description should include (among more obvious duties) the following concerns:

- *Directly manage the institution's board of trustees or board of governors.* For example, whether a board member has been appointed by the governor, is elected by the citizens of the state, or weasels his way onto the board because he is a rich alumnus who thinks he knows something about higher education, the president must devote all the time it takes to make certain the board member is fully informed, is satisfied with the institution's progress, and will not make waves. The president must also be a buffer between the board members and senior staff and faculty. No matter what mistakes a senior administrator might make, or what controversial thing a faculty member might say or do, the president must take responsibility and not allow the board to interfere.

- *Appoint and mentor the best senior staff possible.* For example, there are probably only a dozen administrators in the country who are experts in *both* university finances and student affairs. Just because a person has a doctorate in something or other, or has taken an outrageously expensive Harvard seminar on how to be a university president, that does not make him or her an expert across the board in finances, student affairs, information technology, plant operations, and athletics. Still, a president can and must hire intelligent, earnest, and experienced administrators to see to these various management aspects of a university. And, once those people are on board, the president needs to give them full and unwavering support.

- *Establish a mission statement and maintain an updated strategic plan.* Mission statements and strategic plans go hand in hand. They are dependent on each other. The mission plan points the way; the strategic plan spells out how the mission can be accomplished. In his excellent book *The Creation of the Future: The Role of the American University,* Frank H. T. Rhodes states that a university president's "most important task, and also the most difficult one, is to define the institutional mission and develop its goals. Everything else follows from that; everything else will depend upon it. The mission and goals must be ambitious, distinctive, and relevant to the needs and interests of campus constituents" (p. 223). At least a mission statement is brief and succinct. Strategic plans are much more extensive, and deadly dull to write or update, although there are surprisingly large numbers of university people who enjoy participating in the process. One of those people must be the president, even though he or she may secretly dislike the strategic planning process. The president should demonstrate unbridled enthusiasm, and must insist on a clear mission statement and a comprehensive strategic plan, one that is then widely disseminated and followed.

- *Become an economic guru.* A president probably knows less about economic development than about student affairs or finances or athletics. But this is an area that he cannot delegate to others, though he can certainly ask for advice. Universities today must play an active role in city, regional, and state economic development, as I discuss in chapter 9. Because a great deal of money is usually at stake, the president almost always has to be at the table to contribute to decisions, and to provide leadership to a wide and needy public and political audience.

- *Participate actively in fund-raising.* The securing of significant gifts to the university often requires the president's physical presence. In addition, alumni, athletic supporters, and donors in far-off cities want only to hear the president speak in person. He or she cannot send a surrogate, despite the time and effort that must be expended in grueling travel and idle chitchat.

- *Finally, greet politicians and manage government relations.* The fact of the matter is that there is not one other top administrator in a university who is less able to act on his or her own authority than is the government relations officer. The president has to set policy and make all government relations decisions, but does so on the basis of accurate information and analysis provided by the government relations officer.

A successful university president will be on top of all six of these concerns. Notice that my list makes no mention of the president knowing much about academics, faculty relations, student life, campus security, union contracts, campus construction, or athletics. Certainly, a president should be aware of what is going on, and should be consulted when there are critical decisions to be made, or if a crisis of some sort erupts. But there are of course senior administrators—a provost, vice presidents, legal counsel, and an athletic director, for example—who are directly in charge of these areas and should be able to manage day-to-day operations competently.

So, what is it about those six areas listed above that makes them so important? They are all directly dependent on being led by the president. Each of these areas will succeed (or at least not cause problems) only if the president is in charge. A president is not in charge by e-mail, by memo, or by sending a stand-in, but by leading in person. The president must be the one to pick a staff, talk to board members, greet politicians, and ask alumni for money. No one else can do it. Even if a president stretches the work week to fifty or sixty hours, there will still not be enough time to do all that needs to be done in just those areas.

Unfortunately, few presidents have a governing board chair as understanding as Adele Phelan, of Metropolitan State College of Denver, who writes in the January/February 2009 issue of *Trusteeship:* "In today's competitive world of higher education, in which seemingly no state budgets are at the levels appropriate for a nation that prides itself on valuing higher education, governing boards increasingly are seeking 'entrepreneurial' presidents to diversify revenue streams and otherwise shake up traditional ways of doing business" (page 37). Instead, presidents often have to bury themselves in the minutia of day-to-day matters instead of forging and funding a vision for their institutions.

Politicians at all levels are intimidated by university presidents. I have sat in on numerous committee hearings, from city council to the U.S. Congress, and no person is treated with more respect and deference than a university president. Even when a president makes the stupid choice (or is stupidly so advised by his government relations officer) to testify in favor of an unpopular bill that has no chance of passing, or to comment on the wrong side of a controversial topic, he or she will consistently be addressed politely and listened to patiently.

Why do politicians act this way toward university presidents? Respect for the office? Love of universities? Admiration for the fine jobs those of us at universities are doing educating America's future leaders?

Are you kidding me?

Politicians, the higher up you go (meaning Congress), generally dislike higher education, for theoretical reasons. Conservatives believe higher education is too liberal. Liberals believe higher education does not do enough to promote their causes. Politicians, the lower you go (meaning city and county governments), generally dislike higher education, for practical reasons. Universities demand services and special privileges without being suitably contrite or cooperative about it. Worse, large groups of students can create serious community problems without particularly adding much to the local economy.

Politicians at all levels think that people who work in higher education (especially faculty members) are parsimonious at best. A typical faculty member who has received a $1 million, $5 million, or $10 million earmark because of the direct promotion of the earmark by his or her congressperson would not even dream of paying a hundred dollars to go to a fund-raiser to benefit the congressperson. And woe betide you if you would draw the connection and ask the faculty member to pay up and attend. Presidents are actually somewhat (but not much) more generous than faculty and staff in this regard.

Still, most government relations officers will readily admit that it is easier to get in to see a politician, at any level, if they can tell the politician's staff that the institution's president will be coming along for the visit. There is a variety of reasons why politicians like to see presidents.

First of all, a little bit of glamour rubs off on the politician. Glamour?! Your dowdy president? Actually, that is unfair. Presidents are often attractive people, even as they age. And almost all of them dress very, very well. It is an unspoken but well-recognized fact that one way to climb the ladder in university administration is to buy expensive clothes and know how to wear them. It also helps to drive a sleek and expensive car and not a boxy ten-year old Volvo station wagon. So, besides wearing expensive clothes, why are presidents glamorous? Because they carry the aura of inaccessibility. Most college students never interact with their institution's president, except perhaps shaking hands when receiving their diploma. Out and about in Washington or a state capital, a university president is a rare bird who attracts both attention and respect.

Second, a president brings authority to the meeting with the politician. The visit carries a lot more weight if the president says the university needs a $4 million earmark for a new physics lab and equipment than if the government relations officer or the vice president for research says it. Most politicians do not know or care to know what goes on in a physics lab. But a properly coached president knows at least a little bit. And that is about all it takes. "We need this lab to explore microatoms that will open up an eighth dimension, allowing us to grow taller soybeans," the president says confidently. The politician nods and agrees that big soy beans are good for the economy.

Third, presidents represent universities, and a politician's constituents are very proud that their sons and daughters are attending those universities. A politician does not get a lot of credit at home for helping the dairy industry (unless he is from Wisconsin). No constituent ever comes up to him or her and says, "I'm proud that my kids drink XYZ milk." But many constituents will brag that their kids attend the local university. So, what is more likely to get a politician votes? (A) "I got the dairy industry an extra milk subsidy," or (B) "I got our great local university a new physics lab"?

Fourth, presidents carry their athletic teams around with them. Of course, this carries more weight if the university is playing in the NCAA's Final Four or the Rose Bowl. But this really applies to all levels of university sports and all types of university teams. Why? Because the politicians' constituents—the people back home—care. Even if politicians cannot tell the difference between a free throw and a foul ball, they display in their offices, for visitors to see, at least some sports paraphernalia of the university teams within their political jurisdictions.

Fifth, a politician likes the company of a university president, because she senses that the president is a kindred soul. Lobbyists are loud and boisterous. Advocates are intense and demanding. Business CEOs are overconfident and superior. Staffers are young and clueless. But university presidents are pleasant people, as well as leaders of institutions where knowledge is both valued and created.

Politicians and presidents may get along for another reason, one that probably has no place in a rather formal discussion of higher education and politics, but anyway, here goes. Most politicians and presidents of higher education have a common bond—shyness. No doubt you do not agree, or at least are skeptical. But being out in public and making speeches and so forth does not necessarily mean that you have an extroverted and bubbling personality. Actors, too, often have shy personalities. All three of these professions demand that a person assume a persona more dazzling than himself. They have to *be* a U.S. senator or university president or film star. This persona, especially for the politician or president, runs counter to the long contemplative years of work that got a person to that level. So both politicians and presidents like to think and read and have quiet time—which, ironically, neither profession has. This shyness often surfaces in politicians by the fact that they are poor at small talk. They always want to get down to business and stay on topic, usually hiding the truth that they don't always have appointments and other pending important business to attend to. Presidents are better at small talk. After all, they achieved their positions in part by schmoozing at numerous faculty cocktails parties. Nonetheless, they still like to tell their secretary that they have pressing university business to contemplate while closing their office door to read a scholarly journal article in peace.

The most difficult situation for a government relations officer is to work for a president who is just not interested in politics, and may even be hostile to politicians and the political process. If a president is just disinterested (but not hostile), the government relations officer may be able to work around this apathy. In fact, he or she might welcome being able to work with little oversight and great independence. But this situation, comfortable though it may be, carries a fatal trap for the government relations officer who becomes too complacent, or begins to believe that he or she is really the person running the political show. The government relations officer may assume that he or she need not check with the president first, and eventually makes a critical decision in direct conflict with the president's view or university policy. When that happens just once, the president usually comes to a quick realization that she needs to take control, despite an indifference to politics. And the president may very well decide that perhaps a new face in the office of government relations will make politics more palatable.

A hostile president, in contrast, presents the most difficult situation for the government relations officer. A hostile president often feels superior, and believes that he has a better command of politics than anybody else. This attitude extends beyond the public arena and onto the university campus. These presidents are constantly embroiled in controversy with the faculty's governing body or the athletic director. Just about the only reasonable recourse for the government relations officer in this case is to steer clear of the president as much as possible. Since hostile presidents often have big egos (bigger even than the big egos most university presidents possess), the government relations officer's best strategy is to put this president only in "win" situations. Of course, this is not a bad general policy on how to treat all presidents. But it is hard to pull off all the time, and there are many times when a president's experience and authority can turn a potentially bad situation into a good outcome. Tread lightly with a hostile president, or the bad situation may deteriorate further.

If all else fails in managing a hostile president, a government relations officer may want to tell the president the following true story. Recently, my university hosted a two-week visit of Dr. Iognaid G. O'Muircheartaigh (who fortunately preferred to be called just plain "Iggy"), the recently retired president of the National University of Ireland in Galway. Iggy was a wonderful guest, and a sound advisor to our own president on such matters as economic development. At one point during his visit I asked him if he had much to do with politics. "Oh yes," he replied in his deep Irish brogue. The National University of Ireland receives 85 percent of its income from the government—students do not pay tuition—and that had Iggy spending two or three days *every week* in Dublin, on the other side of Ireland, lobbying for funding. By comparison, asking a hostile president to spend a couple of days a month at the state capital or in Washington should be a breeze.

Fortunately, in this day and age, politically indifferent or even hostile university presidents are rare. And a smart government relations officer should be able to survive until that type of president flames out over some campus issue and a new administration takes over.

What, finally, is the role of a university president in terms of government relations? The answer is simple and can be summed up in three words: money, money, and, oh yes, money. A university president should expend only minimal effort with regard to government where funding is not involved. Certainly, if a congressman calls up and asks to visit for an hour, in order to better understand what the university is doing in regard to medical research, the president should oblige. In truth, such informational visits are rare at best, usually occurring only when someone is first elected.

A spate of new and revised lobbying laws at all levels of government has made the university president's job easier in terms of nonmonetary interactions. There are far fewer calls for the office of the president to grease the wheels for free rounds on the university golf course. Politicians now prefer to meet over a cup of coffee than have to report a breakfast or lunch to an ethics commission. Even most (but not all) sporting events are less attractive.

The bottom line is that it is not particularly difficult for university presidents to restrict their interactions with politicians only to meetings where money is on the line. Let's examine how these political actions may play out by distinguishing different sorts of politicians.

Former Politicians

Former politicians—meaning those who are out of office either because they were defeated in an election or were retired because of term limits— should generally be avoided. Former politicians often become lobbyists, and as lobbyists, they can offer a university little of value and, in fact, can be detrimental to the university. Why? Because they are partisan and seldom, if ever, cross party lines. Former politician lobbyists will push hard to assert that they have access. They might have had access once, but once they leave office, that access generally slips away. Sadly, most of them still think of themselves as players, though the game has passed them by. The danger for a university arises when former politicians use their previous connections or perceived current connection to the university to gain access to current politicians in important offices. Politician lobbyists may also use any connection to a university to impress their lobbying clients. Suddenly, a president is receiving calls from construction contractors or beverage distributors because of a referral from a former politician turned lobbyist.

Politicians who have left office because of term limits or who have suffered an election defeat are less likely to become troublesome but nonetheless must be handled carefully. Some of these politicians simply disappear (literally) or at least return to selling real estate or insurance and are never heard from again, except in newspaper or TV ads promoting their businesses. Still, many term-limited or defeated politicians are relatively young and may resurface in the future as elected officials. They realize that while out of office they have to keep their name in play, so they become members of "study commissions," or are appointed to "regional economic development corporations," or serve as chairpersons of medical fund-raisers.

Others—usually without going through the office of the president—begin teaching part-time at the university, which looks good on a CV. Fortunately, politicians of this inclination are less annoying and dangerous than those who have become lobbyists, because they may face the electorate again and do not want to overstep any official or ethical boundaries. In the end, it is the responsibility of a good government relations officer to keep tabs on all former politicians and inform the president if their actions may have a negative impact on the university.

Local Politicians

University presidents should have as little to do with city and county politicians as possible, because there is nothing to gain and often a great deal to lose. Don't get me wrong. Even at the local level there is money at stake. But the money is usually tied up with more restrictions than an NIH grant. Money available to both public and private colleges and universities sometimes passes from the state or federal governments to local governments. Both city and county governments have access to all sorts of funding, simply because they function as local government units. So, if the federal government decides to initiate a job-training program, it can use the county government structure to distribute the funding. Higher education does job training, of course, and taps into this funding through county governments. This could also be the case for infrastructure grants or other broad federal or state programs.

But this is nitty-gritty business that need not involve the president, except perhaps for a photo opportunity when the university receives a $2 million grant to build streets and sewers in a university technology park adjacent to the campus. Otherwise, in terms of their own money, cities and counties are hard-pressed just to collect the garbage every week and keep the jails open. University presidents should want nothing to do with local funding, especially when the mayor calls and wants the president to endorse a city-operated levy. The operating levy may be completely justified, and the president may understand that its successful passage affects the university, student housing, and surrounding neighborhoods. But offering that endorsement is not the president's job. What's more, the mayor represents one or the other political party, and such an endorsement by a university president may serve only to alienate members of the opposition party.

The reality is that city and county governments do encroach on local universities, no matter how large or small, and the university president must decide who will handle such encroachments. Government relations officers often try to sidestep dealings with local politics. They know that it is down and dirty work that never stops and offers few major victories. Universities, therefore, sometimes create offices of community affairs or the like, which, interestingly enough, often do not even report to government relations offices, but to offices of communications or public relations. There is some logic in this arrangement, because the university's local image is at stake with city/county issues. Nevertheless, a twenty-something university public relations intern cannot be sent to an all-day city zoning meeting where the university is proposing to tear up a local neighborhood in order to build a new dorm. Did anyone say "eminent domain"? I hope not.

Obviously, a university has to be conscious of local politics, and must understand the pitfalls of city/county government relations. But a university president cannot do this work himself, even at a small school. He must create a team of administrators able to handle the multitude of issues that surface at that level. But the president cannot allow his office of government relations simply to absent itself from this work on the premise that there are bigger fish to catch at the state and federal levels. Politics is politics at any level.

State Politicians

State politicians exist either as elected officials or as agency/department heads. Even if an educational institution is not state-supported, its president must establish a relationship with the region's state senators and state representatives, including those who represent the university. This would seem to be a no-brainer, but often it isn't. Besides the fact that all districts are confusingly gerrymandered, block by block and street by street, legislators will go so far as to falsely claim that the university is in their district, or at least that they "represent" the university. Big, sprawling urban universities may indeed be part of more than one district. And branch campuses probably *are* in other districts. The fact is that legislators get a lot of political capital out of representing universities. Universities do not have to get into arguments over who represents them, but the president needs to know the players and the politics in play.

State agency and department heads are generally politicians, either because they served previously in the state legislature or because they are direct appointments by the governor. They are potentially more important to universities than anyone in the state legislature (except for the legislative leadership) because they control agency budgets. Such agencies and departments include (these titles vary, of course, state by state): the Office of the Attorney General; the Department of Development; the Budget Office and Controlling Board;* the Department of Administrative Services, and any or all education departments such as a Board of Regents or the State Board of Education. The university president should get to know well the "politicians" who head all of these agencies and departments.

The person who is both an elected official *and* a department head is the governor of the state. The university president should know and be supportive of the governor, even if his or her personal political views differ. Because the governor cannot play favorites (or at least should not play favorites), she will rarely, if ever, direct funding to an individual campus. But a governor and her staff will clearly establish a tone, by action or inaction, on how the state will help and fund higher education. The president—like all of the presidents of universities in the state—must help the governor establish that tone, and should suggest actions that are beneficial to higher education in the state.

---

* Controlling boards (or similarly named administrative bodies) are usually panels consisting of legislators who are charged with distributing state funds. These men and women authorize the actual writing of checks or, as it is commonly called, the "releasing" of funds. Controlling boards can be extremely political, and in some instances require university representatives to attend every one of their meetings.

How does a university president accomplish that, not only for the governor, but also for state legislators? Let me count (a few) ways:

- Keep in touch. Attend the governor's state-of-the-state speech. Invite him or her to campus. Invite local state legislators to campus.
- Testify before legislative committees. Do this rarely and only on topics that are crucial to higher education in general, or to one's own campus.
- Make absolutely certain that any campus queries from legislators are answered immediately and truthfully. (There are not as many of these questions as one might think, but no matter how trivial, they must be answered.)
- Partner, collaborate, and cooperate with other schools, businesses, social service agencies, and everybody else who is relevant. And make sure all these types of efforts are highly publicized.
- Make certain that the university's government relations officer is well known and is acting for the president as the first campus contact.

Federal Politicians

United States senators and congresspersons have the uncanny ability to make anyone seem like their best friend. Of course, this is a political cliché. But it is true. Because of this "trait," university presidents, who before they became a president typically did not have much contact with political figures, are often seduced by the attention that senators and congresspersons lavish on them. Presidents often mistake this glad-handing for genuine friendship and are certain that these politicians will go out of their way to help the university.

Not true.

Quite frankly, federal elected officials such as congresspersons, senators, and even the president of the United States do not care much about an individual university. Sure, I might be overstating the case. Congresspeople particularly might care if you are the largest university in their district. But believe me—despite what his or her staff member might say to you in private—they do not really care. There are just too many other big issues at stake for them to worry much about your university, Mr. University President.

I know that this seems wrong, and even contradictory to what you and the congressperson talked about at your last face-to-face meeting. I am sure he promised that your earmarks request would receive serious consideration. The congressperson no doubt asked your opinion about some current topics like alternative energy or how to make college affordable. He listened to you intently while an assistant took what appeared to be copious notes.

I hate to break this to you, but neither the congressperson nor the legislative assistant was paying the least bit of attention.

It cannot be overstated that politicians pay attention to the political party they belong to and that got them elected. The party is where a lot of the money will come from when it's time to get them reelected. Certainly it's true that the party structure is not as strong as it once was. Many politicians are comfortable disagreeing in public about various stances of their own party. A liberal Republican may be closer to conservative Democrats than he or she is to conservative Republicans . . . and may vote that way as well. Nevertheless, even though it may be behind closed doors, most politicians are still party loyalists when it comes to the machinations of day-to-day politics.

This is how Washington, D.C., works. When everyone gets together in Washington, issues are often already decided and votes really do not have to be cast. Now there is not one congressperson or senator who would agree with my point of view. They would say that they listen to the folks back home, especially prestigious university presidents. They would argue that they sincerely seek out their constituents' views. They would pledge that they follow their voters' wishes 100 percent of the time.

Or not.

But never mind. The fact remains that university presidents should go to Washington to assert their university's goals and demand (within reason) that their congressperson and senators help. The atmosphere in Washington is electric. The restaurants are excellent. The hotel rooms can cost $500 or more a night. What's not to like? But the sad fact remains that the university president can do little to affect national legislation or gain money for his university that has not already been appropriated by party officials, who often do not even know where the university is located.

University presidents have one of the toughest, if not the very toughest, jobs in America. They make a fair amount of money and they work in nice environments. But the scope of what they have to know and what they have to do rivals that of almost any other job, including politicians'. True, government relations is just one of those jobs, but it is the one job that by itself deals with more money and prestige than any other job. University presidents—even if they have no inclination or desire to— must be conscious of politics and aware of politicians, and must learn to act and react in appropriate ways.

You, You Can Hide

University Faculty

The two young men from Washington were well dressed. Dark suits, white shirts. One wore a red tie and the other wore a blue tie. (Symbolic of the recent presidential election, or simply a coincidence?) They were escorted into the provost's small conference room by the university's vice president for government relations. A dozen professors—all members of the faculty senate's executive committee—were gathered. It was mid-afternoon on a Friday in late autumn.

The young men worked their way around the room shaking hands with the faculty members and apologizing for being a couple of minutes late. Perhaps half of the faculty members had seen the young men before, either when these visitors had spoken previously to faculty groups or, in a couple of cases, when they had met privately to discuss grant applications or political strategy to gain a congressional earmark. It was difficult maneuvering around the room. Chairs banged back against the walls. One of the young men stumbled over a coat that had fallen on the floor. But finally they rejoined the vice president at the front of the room.

This was the men's last meeting of the day before returning to Washington. They had spent a long day on campus: breakfast with the president, lunch with board members, a trip to the university's health science campus, and meetings with researchers and research administrators.

The vice president thanked the faculty for taking time to meet with the young men, to whom he referred by their first names. He did not call them lobbyists or even consultants. They were the university's Washington "contacts." He said the young men would present a brief post-election update and then answer any questions.

The young men began with a personable and chatty analysis of what the election meant, highlighting speculation on where research funding might come from in the next administration. They speculated on possible cabinet members and gossiped about various members of Congress who were either now out of the loop or were about to be in the loop. Questions—as often happens with faculty—were rhetorical and even long-winded at times. But the young men listened patiently. They suggested new avenues of research funding, commented on the potentially increased influence of the local congresswoman, and specifically agreed to meet with one faculty member who wanted to apply for a Department of Defense contract.

After forty-five minutes, the vice president interrupted the conversation and the young men—after shaking hands again around the table—left and headed for the airport. Some of the faculty members lingered, talking in small groups of two or three. They thanked the vice president for setting up the meeting. They were impressed by the young men's style and candor. They liked hearing about goings-on in Washington. The senate president wondered whether the executive committee should make a trip to Washington to meet with the local congresswoman and the state's U.S. senators. The vice president said that could be arranged.

"You know what I liked?" one professor—who was often a critic of the university administration—said. "I liked knowing what's going on. I liked knowing that kind of secret stuff."

Faculty members in American higher education—including community colleges, junior colleges, university branch campuses, public universities, and private universities—are as diverse as the American population. They live in urban centers and rural outposts. They may make a minimal salary or be well-compensated. Some are ambitious, while others are content to put in their years until retirement. They may be interested in sports or opera, or even both. They may never have been sick a day, or might suffer from a chronic illness.

But the approximately 1.7 million faculty members in the United States (that's the number given by the federal Bureau of Labor Statistics) are different from the general populace in two ways.

First of all, they are universally better educated. This goes without saying, since they are known as "college professors" to their own family members (like Great Aunt Harriet, who lives in Milwaukee), to neighbors (like Charley, who lives next door and is a member of the Communications Workers of America), and to their auto mechanic (like Doug, who actually has a higher net income, but vastly inferior health insurance). It is peculiar about the word *professor*. It exists both as a generic term to describe anyone who teaches a college class and as a specific classification designating a senior, tenured faculty member. Many people teach college classes, but the actual number of ranked professors is, of course, very small. The word *tenure* has a similar status. Legislators in particular think just about every college teacher has *tenure*, whereas in reality only about thirty-two percent do, according to the American Association of University Professors.

Second, faculty members tend to be more politically active than the general populace. This fact becomes obscured when election time rolls around and one cannot open a newspaper or turn on the television without being bombarded by ads for candidates. Then everybody seems to be talking politics. But after the election, when most people return to talking about their kids or their cars, or how the local sports teams are doing, faculty members often continue to talk about and think about politicians and political issues.

But if we accept the premise that the faculty are intelligent and politically aware, why then are they often so painfully naïve and ineffective when it comes to hands-on political activity? Clark Kerr believed that faculty members must become more involved in government relations. In the 2002 book *The Future of the City of Intellect: The Changing American University*, he recommends that "faculty governing bodies establish external affairs committees concentrating on relations with government agencies and industry" (p. 15). He declares that a "new age" has arrived, and "a new code might be more oriented to external concerns—in particular on how to protect the university's function as an independent critic of society, on how to guard the integrity of its role as a conscience of society" (pp. 15–16).

I will try to address the question of why post-secondary faculty members are not more effective in addressing political issues by using the remainder of this chapter to profile a half-dozen faculty types. I promise that I will fudge the descriptions just enough that none of your Great Aunt Harriets will recognize you.

The Political Scientist

Question: Where do political scientists hide?
Answer: In their textbooks.

It is logical to assume that the faculty members who teach political science would be the most politically active. Of course this is an error of logic that the general population often makes in regard to university faculty. Few engineering professors spend their weekends building bridges. Few math professors spend their evenings crafting trajectories to send astronauts to Mars. And few education professors drive a school bus every morning. Studying a topic in depth and then having the ability and talent to teach that topic are crucial to the very fabric of our society. But there has always been that gray area between teaching and doing that one hears or reads every once in a while: *Those who can't do, teach.*

So, to our first featured faculty member, the political scientist. I recently attended an annual Master of Public Administration alumni luncheon at my university. Three local state legislators discussed—what else?—politics to the gathering of about 40 people. None of the legislators were alumni of the MPA program but a number of prominent city/county government administrators were. Not only that, but these administrators were more at ease than usual as they chatted and kidded with each other and their former professors. In essence, this gathering was their professional club, and they were pleased to be part of it.

What is important here is that we cannot and must not forget that education is vital to the functioning of government. Most high-profile politicians do not have a political science education. Interestingly, the general public has come to believe that a law degree is somehow a "government education" degree. Certainly, an attorney's training and education may be in a government-related field such as constitutional law, but most attorneys have no particular government administrative expertise.

The task of actually managing governments falls to professionals who are sometimes unfairly categorized as "faceless government bureaucrats." Even politicians divert blame from themselves by criticizing "faceless government bureaucrats," knowing full well that if you do not have a face, it is hard to talk back. The fact is that "faceless government bureau-

What about Consulting?

The irony when faculty members act as consultants (applying their expertise to real-world situations and getting paid for the work) is that they are inevitably criticized for "moonlighting" or "not paying enough attention to their teaching" or even "making too much money." Very often, they must contend with restrictive university consulting rules, to the point where, in some places, they must share earnings with their institution. So sometimes it is not even worth the effort *to do* instead of teach.

crats" are real people who are often underpaid, yet remain dedicated to doing good work for good causes. Lots of these people, especially those who have risen to important managerial posts such as city/county administrators, majored in political science in college.

Even if one acknowledges the importance of providing solid education in how government functions by teaching future government administrators, why don't political scientists on campus have a more influential role in the university's government relations activities? If for no other reason, would not their fundamental interest in politics attract them to university government relations?

The greatest problem that political science faculty members have is compromising their political neutrality. Politics is in all of our faces even in non-election years. Not only is C-Span covering national politics, but most states now have their own state television broadcasts. Since political science courses are not generally part of the required curriculum but are rather electives, only students who have an interest in the subject take them. This fact then tends to make most (but not all) political science faculty members neutral in their teaching roles. They take both sides of the debate. They discuss the theory of government structure behind important issues. They lecture in depth on historical precedents.

In none of this do they do wrong, of course, but neutrality often leads to paralysis, which may mean that political scientists are not active in university relations *away* from the university either. They may not care to participate in the political arena because they may be forced to take a political point of view (the university's) and thus compromise their political neutrality. Still, political scientists often become involved in faculty politics such as the faculty senate, or in union activities such as the American Association of University Professors. They are very effective leaders in these roles, but they are collegial leaders, not political leaders.

Like-minded departments: History, Sociology, Law.

The English Department Radical

Question: Where do English department radicals hide?
Answer: In the past.

An article in *PS: Political Science & Politics* by Mack D. Mariani and Gordon J. Hewitt reports that despite the common belief that liberal professors indoctrinate innocent students, the fact is that students are rarely significantly influenced by their professors' political beliefs. This study marginalizes one of the country's fondest—or most reviled—stereotypes: the bearded English professor in wire-rimmed glasses turning innocent young men into like-minded radicals while bedding innocent young coeds. This is perhaps the most enduring image from the 1960s—besides flowers in your hair or stuck in gun barrels.

Campuses are still populated by bespectacled young English professors and their older colleagues whose long hair is pulled back into thin gray ponytails. Not only is their liberal influence on their students marginal at best, but their political influence is equally marginal. Why is that? After all, an argument certainly could be made that English department faculty are not only the most widely read of all academics, but also perhaps the most culturally aware and sensitive. They tend to be actively and intelligently involved with campus politics ranging the gambit from administrative roles to unions like the AAUP.

Yet no twenty-first-century university president fears an English department political juggernaut the way a university president might have in the sixties.

Why not?

The answer is the lack of unifying causes like the Vietnam War, or the Civil Rights Movement. The English department radical needs a big issue that is supported by university students. Yes, there are global warming, world hunger, economic meltdown, and wars, pretty much around the world. Students certainly have been active in these large issues and in many other smaller issues. But the students have not needed the English professor to rally them to the cause. Students even on the remotest of campuses in North Dakota or Maine are instantly connected with the rest of the world through cell phones, iPods, laptops, and flat-screen TVs, and through Internet networks like Facebook, MySpace, Twitter, and all their cousins. So students feel no particular need to link up with the worldly English professor. But that is not the English professor's only problem. For the past thirty years or more, much of what has gone on in the world has been linked to economics. English professors are smart people, but the reason they went into English instead of finance is that they would rather read books than discuss economic theories. To most of them, reading Thomas Friedman's *The World Is Flat* only confirmed their deep-seated fear that economics—not morality—is running the world.

This gradual shift has led to a general retreat of the English professor from meaningful political action, especially outside academe. Activism has given way to comfort and even golf. Perhaps the English professor will make a comeback if a really, really big (and contentious) issue envelopes the country. But it may be a long wait.

Like-minded departments: Music, Theater, and Art.

The Medical Faculty

Question: Where do medical faculty hide?
Answer: At medical conferences in exotic locales.

Physicians in general are wonderful people, and this is especially true of physicians who are also university faculty members. They are selfless in their service to their communities. They work longer hours than just about anyone else in any other profession. They are dedicated to teaching future health care professionals. They are on the cutting edge of research and often are highly funded. And many of them have made the effort to earn additional degrees in areas such as law and business.

Physicians, however, are part of the American medical profession, which more than any other profession attempts to control and influence all aspects of its practitioners' lives, not just their work. This influence begins during the first days of medical school at the traditional "white coat ceremony," when students are presented a white physician's coat. The coat (which is short, in contrast to the longer white coat worn by a doctor) indicates to a patient that the person wearing it is a medical student and not a *real* doctor. But what it psychologically tells the new students is that the profession will take care of all of their needs, including clothing. It is as much a symbol of profession as it is lifestyle.

The long and rigorous training of medical school often intensifies an unfortunate "us against the world" mentality. As the years go by, students build up huge debts. One might assume that the medical profession would have advocated over the years for legislation to subsidize medical training, or at least to provide extensive scholarships to students, so that this debt would not be so crushing by the time students concluded their residencies. Yet any such advocacy on behalf of students by the profession has been lukewarm at best. At one time in our nation's history, this would have been a no-brainer for politicians to support. That time, however, has long since passed.

Why didn't the profession pursue this benefit? Because it is better for all physicians if medical students emerge from training with debt. These new physicians are immediate converts for any and all legislation to increase physician's pay and reimbursement. And that is the primary motivating factor in all political action: increase physician's pay and government reimbursement in programs such as Medicaid and (primarily) Medicare.

There are 128 medical schools in the United States. Ten of those schools are free-standing, and the rest are part of larger universities. Faculty members in medical schools consider their ultimate boss the dean of medicine and not the president of the university. Therefore their political agenda is set by the dean on behalf of the profession of medicine, and not by the president on behalf of the university. This fact creates all sorts of problems for the president, not the least of which is in the crucial area of research.

Physicians have actually devised an entire category of research that permits them to be paid on many distinct levels. In order to do this they have partnered with two entities that depend upon them: the pharmaceutical industry and the hospital industry. Testing new drugs on humans is necessary. Holding a two-hour seminar, entirely paid for by a pharma-

---

My Only Freebie

When I began my Master's program in English, I received a free copy of *Webster's Seventh New Collegiate Dictionary*. Having a dictionary suddenly appear in my student mailbox one day does not entail the pomp and platitudes of the physician's white coat ceremony, which I have observed many times. Many years later, however, that dictionary is still within arm's reach.

---

ceutical company, to discuss the clinical trial at a Florida resort before adjourning for golf is not necessary. University physicians typically do research that benefits them economically. Therefore, they are not simply useless politically for the university, but actually may be at odds with university policy and mission.

No physician has ever been an American president, and few have been governors, senators, or congressmen—thus an entire cadre of the best and brightest men and women in America are not involved in politics. They are certainly busy providing the best health care in the world, but professionals in many other fields still find the time to contribute to the political process. Many physicians, then, who could be excellent allies for government relations officers, and could be viable advocates for universities in the political arena, are unfortunately disengaged.

Government relations officers at universities with medical schools and/or health science campuses should reach out to physicians and, for that matter, other health care professionals. Both the profession of medicine and the institutions of higher learning, it seems to me, would benefit.

Like-minded department: Engineering.

The Business College Entrepreneur

Question: Where do business college entrepreneurs hide?
Answer: In China.

Like his medical faculty colleagues, the business college faculty entrepreneur's main priority is to make money. But there are two crucial differences that make the entrepreneur more of a university team player than is his medical counterpart. One difference is that there are many more business schools than there are medical schools. As a result, business schools tend to be better integrated into the various faculty and administrative systems of the university. The second, most important, difference is that the entrepreneur has figured out how to use the political system for his or her benefit.

Entrepreneurs smell money just about everywhere. While most university budgets reserve money for personnel and student instruction, there are still pockets of cash that entrepreneurs are particularly adept at sniffing out. One strategy that is used with particular effectiveness by business college entrepreneurs is the creation of centers, or institutes. Of course there are lots of centers and institutes, especially at large universities. But most of these centers have academic roots (not surprisingly) and depend on mercurial university funding or the usually small annual interest of a one-time gift or donation. Business college centers tend to be managed more proactively. They have aggressive names like "The Center for Small Business Success" or "The Institute for Business Innovation." Such centers are often established in partnership with successful local and sometimes even national businesses that often provide annual support funding.

On the one hand, business college centers exist chiefly as conduits for business faculty to consult about a multitude of topics, such as business planning, personnel and benefit management, supply chain strategies, and international business opportunities. Like physician practice plans, business faculty have managed to link making personal income with an academic mission. They have accomplished this by developing business cooperative and internship opportunities for students as a by-product of their consulting. These "real world" experiences are always enthusiastically endorsed by university administration, despite the irony that these co-ops and internships are occasionally poorly vetted and supervised. (Just because someone is successful in business does not make him an effective business professor. More than a few students end up being "gophers," operating under the rationalization that they are learning the business "from the bottom up.")

Business faculties also discovered, early on, that *all* levels of government, from city/county to state to federal to international, provide mechanisms for economic development funding. This funding varies widely in terms of names, amounts of money available, and purpose. For example, a state might create a "Technology Incubator Start-up Program" funded through the state's Office of Development. Although most university faculty would shrink away from the paperwork and bureaucracy of applying for what might be a modest amount of money, business college entrepreneurs plunge right in, and will more often than not come away with an award. The money is out there.

To facilitate such success, business college entrepreneurs have become more politically savvy than have their colleagues. They know politicians. They keep track of business issues. They attract donors. And they know how to dress up in expensive suits to impress people. All of this has an important fallout for university politics. Business programs are aimed at demonstrable successes. Successes can be used by university officials to demonstrate to elected officials that money *given* to the university is actually money *invested* in the university. There is a return to government in terms of new businesses, more tax revenue, and higher employment.

And, if a business college entrepreneur convinces a Chinese widget company to locate a new plant in the state, that's a win-win for everybody.

Like-minded departments: Economics and Marketing.

The College of Education Faculty

Question: Where do college of education faculty hide?
Answer: In the public schools.

Among other things, colleges of education teach students how to be grade school teachers, and high school teachers, and school administrators. There is very little variation among universities from the K–12 mission, except for some graduate programs in higher education administration. This is the most obvious and straightforward mission of any university academic unit. It has always been a very public mission, because pretty much every person in America goes to school, and almost all school funding comes from local and state taxes. Therefore, politicians can rightly and appropriately assert that they should have a say on how colleges of education teach the teachers. *Intelligent design, anyone?*

Historically, to counter and obviate this political pressure, education professors developed pedagogy. Pedagogy is defined by the dictionary as the "art, science, and profession of teaching." In other words, to avoid having politicians tell education professors what they should be teaching students to teach, the education professors claim that they only teach teachers *how* to teach, not *what* to teach. Confused politicians generally have accepted this claim.

This cozy arrangement has worked for decades for colleges of education, and colleges of education became almost untouchable fortresses within universities. They had a steady stream of students whom they captured early in their student years by means of rigid curricula that began as freshmen. College of education graduates were practically guaranteed jobs, and a good number of these graduates returned to campus for masters and even doctorate degrees. If a small state university or private university had any graduate programs at all, they were almost always in education.

But a perfect storm of societal changes over the past twenty years has stressed the comfortable existence enjoyed in colleges of education. There has been a crisis in K–12 funding as local and state economies have declined. Parents and politicians are asking why students in K–12 are not better educated, and do not do better on national tests. There has been a nationwide movement to establish charter schools, which claim to provide better alternative education in a private setting while using state funding. More students are considering careers in education because of job guarantees, but ironically, many jobs in education are disappearing. Computer technology has revolutionized classroom instruction all the way down to the lowest grade levels. And university administrations, even at former state teacher colleges, have realized that colleges of education, with their large numbers of expensive senior faculty members, may not be the profit centers they once were.

Colleges of education have been slow to react politically, perhaps because they are often staffed with senior faculty members who are generally opposed to change. College of education faculty are strongly influenced by national and state professional associations that accredit education programs. These associations tend to be conservative and reactionary in nature. They resist change adamantly, and repeat over and over to legislators that the trained educators know best how to teach. Frustrated legislators, however, in state after state, have rejected this argument and have altered school funding by creating charter school systems, establishing statewide testing programs, and even legislatively revamping K–12 curricula, often under technology guidelines (the disciplines of science, technology, engineering, and math, also known as STEM fields).

For many years, universities ignored this rising crisis in K–12 education. An admissions office did not care if a qualified student came from a charter school or a public school. Of course, the key word in the last sentence is "qualified." As universities started to lower admission requirements in order to maintain enrollment numbers, they became more interested in what was going on in K–12 education. College of education deans and faculty—rightly or wrongly—asserted that their primary mission was to prepare teachers. They did not engage in political battles advocating for passage of local school levies, or preventing the imposition of state K–12 testing. They resisted getting pulled into the societal and political battles that raged across communities and states concerning primary and secondary education.

This is an enormously complicated issue, one that goes to the heart of America's future. Universities are going to have to spend more of their campus resources and their political capital if they are to cope with the problems of K–12 education. Somewhere along the line, the colleges of education faculty members will have to get out of the public school classroom and into the public fray.

Like-minded departments: Some university administrations.

The Research Scientist

Question: Where do research scientists hide?
Answer: In Washington, D.C.

Research scientists are the most politically active faculty members in American universities. And universities are just fine with that arrangement, as long as the grant funding from Washington continues.

Research scientists bring in millions of dollars to universities, sometimes tens of millions of dollars. But research scientists are less demanding than medical faculty, business faculty, and even other totally nonproductive faculty members in the liberal arts. They persist against incredible odds to obtain grants from the National Science Foundation (NSF), the National Institutes of Health (NIH), the Department of Defense, and other grant sources. These highly lucrative grants not only fund research but also supply universities with indirect cost funding, generally in excess of forty percent of the total grant.

Research scientists understand one basic political rule that few if any other faculty members understand: persistence pays off. They are willing to submit grant applications year after year until they are successful. They are willing to go to Washington over and over again to explain their research projects to congresspersons who are only half-listening at best. They are willing to toil in the most miserable conditions of anyone in the university for years until their grant is finally funded and they can build their ideal laboratory.

Research scientists are polite and humble, and seldom argue with university administrators, unless the administrators do something stupid like decide to take away lab space. Not that research scientists—especially the consistently well-funded ones—cannot be arrogant at times. They have an annoying tendency to think that politicians are their friends, and that they fund their projects out of a love for science, rather than for the more venal reason of just wanting to get their share of the earmark pot. Then again, who cares, as long as the funding ultimately comes to the university?

It is not just by chance that the highest-rated universities in America are also the ones that have the most research scientists and the most research funding. Research scientists can certainly make a government relations officer's life easier and more successful. But they must be constantly monitored from a political point of view, lest they step outside the parameters of their grants and foul up a good deal.

Like-minded faculty: Unfortunately, almost no one.

The Other Faculty, and Methods of Engagement

These above portraits of university faculty highlight only some of the many faculty groups who do or do not have effective political connections.

There are many individual faculty members who have outstanding and important political connections. An economics professor may be an advisor to the governor on the state's economy. A history professor may write a column on politics for a national newspaper. A sociology professor may be a commentator for National Public Radio. Or, a biology/environment professor may head a Green task force for the city's mayor. In addition, entire disciplines are making efforts to become more hands-on politically. An article by David Glenn in the September 21, 2009, issue of *The Chronicle of Higher Education* describes a movement among political scientists that involves immersive field work where faculty involve themselves in everyday social/political activities.

Faculty members are indeed active in political life. But it takes consistent contact with them if one is to understand and be aware of everything that may be of mutual interest. Most of the time, faculty members' political efforts benefit the university. But not always. A government relations officer should stay informed about what faculty members are doing, either as a group or individually. Talking to deans and provosts is one way to stay connected. Attending faculty senate meetings and reading internal university publications is another. Bringing the university's Washington "contacts" to campus to speak to the faculty senate's executive committee is a good idea. Cynthia Wilbanks, vice president of government relations at the University of Michigan, recommends creating a government relations faculty advisory committee (see chapter 10). Any or all of these efforts will help a government relations officer and staff stay apprised of faculty political attitudes, efforts, and successes. Doing so may actually convince some of them that the government relations office may occasionally provide consequential help.

CHAPTER THREE

Enmesh

Local Governments

While surfing the Internet one day I came across the mission statement for the Office of Government Relations at the University of Kansas: "As a public university, the University of Kansas works closely with the Kansas Legislature, Governor's Office, the U.S. Congress, and federal agencies. The Office of Government Relations provides information to legislators and government officials about the university's positions and policies that improve KU's education mission in Kansas."

Despite having a mission to improve education in the state, there is virtually no mention of the University of Kansas's home in the city of Lawrence. In fact, the only way you get to anything about Lawrence, Kansas, is through the university's Web search engine. The Applied English Center site has a link to the city's Web site, but there is no information about the surrounding community.

It would seem that the relationship between the university and the local governments is so strong that no one has to worry about any local problems. The city's brief 2007 Annual Report barely mentions the large national university in the middle of town. Perhaps relations are so good that the university's government relations staff can ignore local politics and concentrate on state politics down the road in Topeka, and on national politics in Washington. It's good to know that there is at least one university in America that has excellent relations with both its city and county governments.

But despite this seemingly peaceful existence, a recent editorial in the May 18, 2008, issue of the newspaper *Lawrence Journal-World* began as follows:

It's relatively simple for state universities—and particularly, it seems, Kansas University—to say "we need" more money to operate our schools. But no matter how they try to justify tuition increases to provide that funding, there is little doubt that they increasingly are placing a university education out of reach for many Kansas students. At last week's meeting of the Kansas Board of Regents, the state's six universities presented proposals for fall tuition increases that ranged from 1.9 percent to 8.4 percent. Guess who was at the top? You've got it: KU.

What? Perhaps the faithful and obedient citizenry of Lawrence are a little bit upset that the university might be gouging some of the hometown students? Basketball championships notwithstanding, whose responsibility is it to talk to the paper's editorial board, and to soothe the ruffled Jayhawk feathers of local officials?

This is the job of the university's government relations officers—unless, of course, they are spending the day in Topeka or the week in Washington.

Local Politics

There is no glamour in dealing with city and county politics. It is brutal work, and it goes on all day, every day, for 365 days a year. There are few rewards—although that is changing somewhat—and many pitfalls. There is nothing more boring than sitting through a zoning hearing, or a county commissioners' meeting. But someone has to do it, unless you naively believe that city and county officials will always act with your university's best interests at heart. Even if city and county officials support a university project, potential dangers linger.

For example, the University of Toledo recently sold a small off-campus piece of land to the national Red Cross. The Red Cross planned to add a warehouse to an existing vacant building to create a three-state blood distribution center that would eventually add 200 new jobs to the region. Just prior to the needed zoning change, *one* neighbor made *one* phone call to *one* city councilman. The neighbor mistakenly believed that the new building was going to be a blood collection center, as opposed to a blood distribution center. (The councilman, unfortunately, professed ignorance of the proposed center or its purpose.) But that one phone call blocked the zoning change and the sale of the property in its tracks, necessitating a full-scale zoning hearing in council chambers, attended by numerous city councilpersons and staff as well as many university administrators (but no neighbors). The result was that the zoning change was approved, but with the proviso that the university hold two separate meetings with neighbors to explain the situation. Both meetings were duly held, again with heavy attendance by elected officials and university administrators, and . . . no neighbors.

Did the university, including me and my government relations staff, drop the ball? The answer, as it often is in politics, is yes and no. In the Red Cross zoning case, there was no requirement to hold a neighborhood meeting. The university followed all the zoning requirements to the letter. There were even a couple of articles in the city newspaper publicizing the new building and the jobs that would be created. The new building, however, was near a neighborhood that borders the campus. Although the university had no plans to acquire property in that neighborhood, the very idea that a new university building (the warehouse addition) was going up was enough to panic at least one homeowner into calling the city council. Should the university have gone door to door handing out pamphlets explaining the property sale? Or would that action have elicited even more of a reaction? Should we have planned our own neighborhood meeting without being told to by the city? Or would that have just encouraged more rumors? These challenges with the Red Cross land deal illustrate the enmeshed nature of universities and their local governments.

The administrator for the county commissioners in the county where my university is located once told me that the county contains more than fifty different political jurisdictions, which can be defined as organized groups of appointed or elected officials spending money for the public welfare. Our county includes a large city, suburban towns, and some rural land. So, besides the county commissioners, there are city councils, township trustees, public school districts with school boards, water districts, park districts, and various judicial systems.

Just to demonstrate how complicated local government can get, consider the concept of townships. The pilgrims brought the idea of township government to the New World, and today there are twenty-two states (mostly in New England and the upper Midwest) that have township (sometimes just called "town") governments. Townships are parcels of land that were mostly established by Congress in territories before those territories became states. For example, Ohio has 1,309 townships inside the state's 88 counties. Each township in Ohio has three elected trustees who manage a government that parallels county and city governments, including functions such as road maintenance, police and fire protection, parks, cemeteries, and zoning.

Every university, regardless of its size and location, is enmeshed in some if not all of these various political jurisdictions. Fortunately, a university's interaction with many of these jurisdictions may be relatively minimal: a university may be exempt from paying taxes; it may not be located close to any existing parks. It may not have to support a school levy publicly (although I bet the university will be asked). But other local political jurisdictions have a profound effect on a university. Take water, for example. Water is a precious commodity, one that we often take for granted because of its relatively cheap availability. A university must buy water for its campus, just like individuals must do for their homes. But what if there are multiple residence hall complexes on campus? Water is an indispensable need for all universities. And when an indispensable need is provided by a single provider, you tend to pay dearly for it. But how many of you know who negotiates water rates for your university?

Another jurisdictional factor for both cities and counties is the local police force. Generally, three separate police forces are involved with any institution of higher education: the city or town police, the county sheriff department, and the state highway patrol. And other police/security forces may appear on campus for various reasons. These include but are not limited to the FBI, the Secret Service, the DEA, Homeland Security, the State National Guard, and federal troops.

The university's first line of interaction with all of these police forces is the university's own police or security force. Especially since the terrorist attacks of September 11 and the recent spate of campus violence, universities have devoted enormous amounts of time and money to campus security and crime prevention. New alert systems are just high-profile examples of the complex meshing of on- and off-campus policing that has gone on for decades. Off-campus partying in city neighborhoods. On-

campus drug busts. Sexual violence on and off campus. Parking viola-
tions on city streets surrounding a campus. Binge drinking. The list goes
on and on, and for every suspected and actual crime, campus police have
to interact with one or more of the off-campus police or security forces
listed above.

Local Politicians

Mayors, often lonely and isolated people, are very similar to university
presidents. Other politicians, like state legislators, can escape to the state
capital to parlay with their cronies, and members of Congress can fly off
to the excitement of Washington. But like a university president, the
mayor is mostly stuck at home managing a complex social and governmental structure. Mayors and presidents are both accountable to a broad
populous base that includes many people who believe they could do their
jobs better. In addition, both mayors and presidents report to citizen
groups—city councils and governing boards—who consider themselves
to be peers.

Mayors like to associate with university presidents in and around their
cities, but university presidents tend to be less enamored with their mayors. A mayor has everything to gain by being seen with a university president; a university president has everything to lose by being seen with a
mayor. Alongside the university president, the mayor gains an intellectual aura, association with winning athletic teams, and access to university experts and expertise. Next to the mayor, the president runs the risk
of alienating the other political party in town, being mocked by his or
her own faculty, and receiving calls from campus neighbors complaining
about garbage collection or snow removal. Nevertheless, mayors and presidents exist in a symbiotic relationship. They depend on each other not
only because of proximity, and because universities use city services, but
also because of today's increasing need for cooperation in economic development. Many larger universities (and many smaller ones) have tried
to emulate the famous Research Triangle Park in North Carolina (or Silicon Valley, for that matter). What self-respecting university does not have
its own research park? Faculty researchers and trustees love the concept,
and mayors do, too. From the mayor's point of view, the university bears

all the expense of developing the technology park, while the city gains businesses and tax revenues. Cities in this situation usually demonstrate their support by offering modest infrastructure upgrades, just as long as there is adequate media coverage of the ribbon-cutting ceremony.

University presidents and their government relations staff view the mayor's office as a politically dead-end job. Only one big-city mayor, Grover Cleveland, has risen to the office of U.S. president. Few mayors become governors or senators or even congresspersons. The U.S. Council of Mayors states that its membership includes 1,100 mayors of towns with populations of 30,000 or more. But despite their large numbers, mayors do not get out much. They are busy with garbage collection and snow clearing. They deal with construction permits and greedy utility companies. They worry about downtown development and hotel taxes. Because of the daily pressures of the job, and because mayoral offices may not be subject to much oversight, mayors sometimes misuse their power. They may hire family and friends to work for the city. They may be at odds with the city's chief of police. They may threaten to withhold vital services to suburbs and surrounding communities despite signed agreements, or they may threaten to annex those same suburbs and surrounding communities.

Recognizing the dead-end nature of their positions, mayors tend to be poor compromisers. Mayors cannot provide state subsidies, state research and scholarship funding, or federal earmarks, so they and their cities may have little to contribute to the academic mission of universities. But universities clearly enhance city reputations and attract people who receive good salaries. Still, universities can take their city settings for granted, and that makes mayors mad. Mad mayors may raise water and sewer rates, or throw up roadblocks to zoning changes, or cause problems for students living off-campus. So how does a university president or a government relations officer handle an uncooperative mayor?

A university has two strategies for dealing with a truculent mayor. The first is to ally with enough elected city officials to at least neutralize the mayor. The second strategy is to use the media strategically, because mayors hate bad publicity more than any other politician does. But both of these strategies can backfire on the institution. They obviously should be used with caution, and only if the situation is dire or may become dire.

The first strategy involves elected bodies such as city or town councils. There are thousands upon thousands of such governing bodies in America. They come in all sizes and shapes, from formal big-city deliberative bodies to small-town New England–style meetings. Sometimes the elected councilpersons represent the citizens in particular sections or districts of a city; sometime they represent the entire population. In my university's city, six councilpersons represent districts and six represent the whole city. Sometimes the mayor chairs the council, and sometimes the council elects its own leader. Whatever their size and configuration, the one thing true about all city councils is that they like to *mull over* the issue of the day.

"Mull" is a popular word for newspaper headline writers because it is short and has a precise meaning. For example, "City Council *mulls* annexation try" or "City Council *mulls* Mayor's budget." Meaning "to grind out; to pulverize," mull is exactly what a city council does best. It grinds out and pulverizes whatever issue it addresses. Despite the fact that most city councils meet regularly throughout the year, they move with the speed of a tortoise taking a nap.

The problem with city/town council members is that they take seriously their role of representing all of their electorate. State and federal politicians have the luxury of ignoring huge swaths of the people because their districts are large and they spend a lot of time away from their districts at the state capital and in Washington. But city councilpersons get elected precisely because they are neighbors, and they promote that fact to the voters. A congressperson says to the voters, "I want you to send me to Washington so I can promote democracy around the world." A city councilperson says to the voters, "I want you to send me to City Hall so our streets will be plowed on time." So, when you are unable to go to work because of snow drifts in your street, whom are you going to call?

At the time of this writing, the main campus of my university is in the city district of a councilwoman who lives just two blocks from campus in a predominantly minority neighborhood. In meetings, she has asked for some promises from the university. She does not want the university to use eminent domain to wipe out her neighborhood. As a corollary to that promise, she wants the university to also promise that it will control the types of businesses that populate the heavily used city street that separates the campus from her neighborhood. These promises are not hard for the university to keep. We have absolutely no intention of invading the neighborhood under the guise of eminent domain. We share an interest in upgrading the stores and restaurants on the street between the campus and the neighborhood. What the university gets in return from our un-official pact with our councilwoman is an ally on the city council (as well as an ally in the minority community, which is just as relevant). The councilwoman serves on important council committees, including zoning, and since she is in the same party as the mayor, she can carry our message to him when necessary. It is one small way the university has to neutralize ideas from the mayor that have the potential to be detrimental to the university.

But understand that this simple pact came about after months of meetings and negotiations. The president has several times invited the councilwoman to his office for coffee, and she is invited to precisely one football game per year in the president's suite. The government relations staff continues to meet regularly with her and with the neighbors. This all takes a lot of time and patience, but the mutual benefits that emerge are worth it.

The continuing effort with the councilwomen that I just described must be repeated concurrently with the other eleven councilpersons in our city. Certainly, not every other councilperson is as interested in the university as is our own councilwoman. But all of them do have interests of various kinds that intersect directly and indirectly with the interests of the university. For example, a few of them are very strong union supporters, and the university has seven different unions among its employees. A couple of council members, including the council's president, are out in front on economic development, and believe the university is obligated to be a leader in the city's economic development. Other councilpersons are interested in the public school system, and believe the university should do more in bolstering the local schools.

Beyond all of these issues, the university has also to remember that the city council listens to the neighbors and friends who elected them. Council members often communicate to us what the people of the city think of us. We cannot ignore them. By paying them considerate attention and by being truthful, the university will find the city council of great help, especially in its relationship with the mayor.

The second way to improve relations with the mayor is through the local media. To paraphrase the late politician Tip O'Neill, besides *USA Today*, the *New York Times*, and the *Washington Post*, all media is local. By media, I primarily mean newspapers, which exist in virtually every town that has a university. Larger cities often have television stations as well, but local television stations are so understaffed that they are unable to cover the university in much depth, except for sports coverage and an occasional "feel good" story fed it by the university media relations people. Newspapers are different, however. Newspapers are read widely (particularly by politicians) and can do more than any other media outlet to shape the public image of the university. They are also difficult to manipulate. They are aggressive in ferreting out "bad news" stories. And they offer their own opinions through editorials, and print their readers' opinions in letters to the editor.

Media matters are usually the job of a university's communications department or public relations office. Government relations officers often have love-hate relationships with their university colleagues in communications. A government relations officer tends to slip into acting like a politician's press agent when the politician visits campus: Why didn't communications issue a press release? Where was the photographer? Why can't the campus newspaper write a story about the visit? *"I promised the congresswoman's chief of staff that we would have some press coverage!"* I have found myself whining to our vice president for communications. *"What's the matter with your people?"*

Of course, nothing is the matter with the university's communications people. They are just doing their jobs, which is a lot more complicated than writing about and photographing a politician wandering around campus. Is there anything duller than one more photo of the university president shaking hands with our long-serving congresswoman? The vice president of communications points out that unless the congresswoman is presenting at least a six-figure check to the president, the situation is not newsworthy.

A university government relations office must devise a viable communications strategy. This strategy must address both state and federal politicians, but its main focus should be on local government and the university, and the strategy must presume that all media is local. A successful communications strategy starts with seven steps:

1. Clearly establish five to ten local political goals that the university hopes to accomplish over the next one to two years. These goals can be gleaned through conversations with the president and senior leadership, and by understanding the university's published mission and strategic plan. Such goals include recruitment of more local minority students, better cooperation between campus police and local police, expansion of the university technology park, and upgrading of the sewer system serving the university. (Okay, so maybe a new sewer isn't mentioned in the university's mission statement, but you get the idea.)

2. Analyze the attitudes, if known, of the mayor and the city administration toward the university goals that you have identified. Rank the goals as to which ones are realistic to achieve and which ones might be thwarted by such things as finances. Also, identify negative issues that the mayor might have with the university.

3. Repeat this analysis with the members of the city/town council.

4. Repeat steps 2 and 3 above, analyzing the county and the county commissioners if relevant to your institution.

5. Identify external organizations or institutions in the city, and such issues as may impact the university. One constant might be an independent economic development group such as the port authority.

6. Discuss how the media in the city (concentrating on the newspaper, or the most influential newspaper if your city has more than one) will cover the major issues that you have identified in steps 1 through 4.

7. Develop a political strategy and share it with the president, senior leadership including academic leadership, and the office of communications. Then implement the plan and update the plan at least once every three months.

Remember: No one else at the university will have thought of doing this. Universities are notoriously reactive rather than proactive in regard to local politics. Therefore, many people, especially in senior leadership and faculty ranks, will be surprised at the breadth of your list. Use this surprise to your advantage in demonstrating the importance of managing government relations at the local level.

Mise-en-Scène

Everyone in the president's office is on high alert. Food service has delivered coffee and breakfast rolls. University administrators involved in the meeting—including the vice president for government relations, the assistant to the president for economic development, and the vice president for research—have arrived early, and are going over notes in the outer office. The president comes out of his office to remind his secretary to hold his calls. The receptionist finds her stamp, by which to validate the visitor's parking tickets.

Everyone, including the president, switches their cell phones to vibrate.

Who are these important guests? Are they major donors? United States senators? The governor and his chief of staff? Even the mayor and members of the city council?

None of the above. They are the county commissioners.

Who?

Why are the faceless and nameless bureaucrats who run the amorphous shadow government that functions behind the scenes of the county's various city governments deserving of all this attention? What in the world is going on here?

There are several one-word answers to why the president and top administrators of a large urban university are catering to county commissioners: Money. Services. Location.

We usually think about contemporary politics in terms of taxes, elections, wars, the economy, Social Security, and, of course, NIH grants. But the history of politics inevitably goes back to land—who owns it, who builds and farms on it, who divides it up and taxes it. Inside every state, most land is divided into counties. Alaska calls its counties boroughs. Louisiana calls its counties parishes. And the five boroughs of New York City are actually counties of New York state, which otherwise uses the word "county." Most of the more than 3,100 counties in America have their own system of government, run by elected commissioners (sometimes trustees) and managed by an appointed (or elected) administrator or executive.

Counties control land, and over the decades counties have funded large public institutions situated on that land. The television show *ER* takes place in County General Hospital, modeled after the famous Cook County Hospital in Chicago. Before naming rights became a profitable alternative, many sports stadiums had "county" in their names, like the Atlanta Braves Fulton County Stadium. Seattle's King County International Airport is one of many airports that incorporate the word "county" in their names. Like these examples, universities occupy lots of land, and thus are subject to county rules such as zoning ordinances, utility agreements, and infrastructure restrictions.

Most cities, towns, and villages also sit on county land, although there are at least three dozen larger cities that are independent of their surrounding counties. Since counties are governmental units, they duplicate similar municipal services. One of the most obvious of these services is law enforcement. Cities have police chiefs, policemen, and city jails. Counties have sheriffs, deputies, and county jails. Counties also have a tax structure, and they have their own highway systems. The list goes on and on, and depending on the location may include garbage collection, a countywide school district and superintendent staff, and so forth. Therefore, cities and counties must cooperate to provide complementary and cooperative government.

Sometimes they cooperate, that is. Often, as one might expect when two similar entities exist simultaneously in the same place (think about your brother-in-law and his family moving permanently into your house), problems occur. Seemingly small problems can become big problems for a university caught in the crossfire. University attorneys are often called upon to resolve the resulting problems that are legal in nature. Government relations officers have to work out many more problems, as well as devote time and effort to preventing them.

One of the most important issues in today's society has to do with economic development. Whether a state has 254 counties (Texas) or only 5 (Rhode Island and Hawaii), county governments around the country have become increasingly active players in economic development. Again, it goes back to the land. Counties almost always have access to land that can be set aside for business or industry development. Cities, on the other hand, seldom have access to open and inexpensive land within their limits. In addition, because the counties in a state account for most of the land, state and federal governments dole out certain funding that is intended to reach all the citizens of the state and nation. For example, state workforce development under federal funding is often distributed through the counties as well as to cities and states. In consequence, counties and county commissioners behind the scenes and mostly under the media radar use their muscle to promote job creation, which is the core of economic development.

So, let's see what happened in the president's office when the three county commissioners arrived.

The three commissioners are all from the same political party. They validate their parking tickets and joke that maybe the county should build the university a new parking garage, so as to help alleviate the university's notorious reputation for lacking adequate parking. There is nervous laughter, since that is exactly what the university would like the commissioners to do. But on this day, the commissioners have their thoughts on a different matter. One of the county's economic development agencies has a hot lead on a biotech industry that would mean a couple of hundred jobs and lots of money for the region. But the company needs a connection to university research, including offices and at least two laboratories.

"If the university funded a couple of lab technicians, that would be helpful as well," a commissioner suggests.

Hiring lab techs and giving up research space makes the president pale. The vice president for research looks positively sick. Negotiations begin, and drag out through the morning. The commissioners claim that the company is projecting a half a million to a million dollars in research investment to the university. The president calls in the provost, while the commissioners summon the head of their economic development agency. Eventually, the president's assistant is asked to order sandwiches for lunch.

In the end, a compromise is reached. The university promises a couple of offices and one lab with one technician, in a building that is being renovated. Since space is not yet assigned, no faculty member will be displaced. That is a big break for the university. And the building will not be finished for six months, which is about the time the new company will be relocating—if, of course, the mayor follows through on his promise to the commissioners that the city will grant the company a five-year tax abatement. Finally, the commissioners leave, with handshakes all around and more jokes about university parking.

So here is my recommendation. A university office of government relations must have at least one full-time staff member who deals with nothing but local governments. This is not a community activity person arranging for the president to participate in chamber of commerce golf outings. This is a person who is actively interested in sitting through city council sessions and is willing to memorize the names of the county commissioners. This person must be well known to the community, and must be featured conspicuously on the university Web site, so that local government officials can access him or her. This person will save everyone, on both sides of the fence, a lot of grief. Are you paying attention, Kansas?

CHAPTER FOUR

Ensnare

State Governments

Poll: State voters averse to altering legislative term limits

—March 1, 2008, *Toledo Blade*

For state legislators, two political priorities are more important than anything else in their profession. The first priority is to get reelected to their current office, elected to a more prestigious political office, or be appointed to a state government job. The second priority is to be loyal to their political party. Every word spoken or action taken by a state legislator comes after the legislator has taken into consideration these two priorities and has modified his or her words or actions accordingly. These two priorities apply to all politicians, from township trustees to the president of the United States. Yet they particularly apply to state legislators and the complex intertwining of state government with both public and private higher education. A closer examination of these two priorities will help explain how the state manages to *ensnare* university boards, administrations, faculty, and students.

Since the 1990s, twenty-one states have experimented with term-limit statutes for legislators. Since then, six states have repealed term-limit legislation by either legislative action (two) or state supreme court rulings (four). Of course, Congress does not have term limits, even though the concept is widely supported by the electorate. The popularity of term limits creates a dilemma for legislators, who intensely dislike the concept.

Publicly, legislators dislike term limits because they are in and then out of office before they are able to thoroughly understand and negotiate complex government issues. Legislators argue that they must increasingly depend on interest groups and lobbyists to sort out these issues. Therefore, the concept of term limits as forcing unnecessary legislative turnover has the effect of increasing the influence of special interests, including higher education.

Privately, legislators oppose term limits because of the lack of job security. They cannot make politics their career simply by being forever reelected to a safe seat. So legislators, once elected in term-limited states, immediately start angling for some other political office or state government job. Of course, legislators do this to some extent in non-term-limited states as well. It is the nature of the beast. But there is no such thing as a "safe seat" in term-limited states, and no politician can remain for years as a Speaker of the House or chair of the Senate education committee. Term limits dramatically change the dynamics of the legislature, if for no other reason than by making the legislators serving in leadership roles substantially younger.

In states with term limits, higher education leaders are constantly trying to determine which legislators favor university support and which do not. Key committee chairmanships change rapidly. A constant danger is that new members often support higher education in principle—and often voice that opinion—before the realities of the state budget, construction bonds, and letters from parents about high tuition costs set in. Neophyte politicians often do not admit to government relations officers or other higher education lobbyists that their support is wavering.

Where does higher education get beat up the most? In a place where neither you nor I have ever been (unless you are an ex-legislator). That place is the party caucus. Those of us who hang around the chambers of a statehouse get used to the abrupt and often inexplicable disappearance of all the legislators from one party. Sometimes the legislators from both parties are simply gone. Within minutes or even seconds, the whispering begins: "They're caucusing!" echoes off the marble walls. The government relations officers exchange glances. *Are they talking about us?* No one is quite sure. And then, just as mysteriously, they are all back in their seats and the committee hearing or session resumes as if nothing has happened.

It is appropriate to be paranoid about what exactly does happen in the party caucus. Legislators generally pledge not to discuss the issues that are debated there. If asked, they will probably say that it was a party matter—such as concerns about loyalty and making sure they have the votes. But it is naïve to take that explanation at face value. What really happens in caucus is yelling and screaming. At least a little bit. It is akin to what happens in grand juries, where the prosecution gets to present its case without necessarily offering all the facts, and without any opposing argument. Moreover, the parties involved are usually quick to jump on some bandwagon or other. If one legislator expresses disappointment in a state university because a constituent has complained about rising tuition, the other legislators of his/her party aren't likely to defend the university. When government relations officers visit the state capitol, they aim to present as much germane information about their school as possible, so that when they are not around, or when legislators are in caucus, there at least will be some seeds of university support in legislators' minds.

Term limits apply to only 30 percent of the states. But party caucuses happen everywhere and often, and as a political procedure they are difficult if not impossible for an outsider to significantly influence. So why do I have term limits and caucuses introducing a chapter on state legislators and universities? Because they can help us understand the character of the 7,382 men and women who are state legislators. More than any other politicians—except, perhaps, for extremely popular and/or powerful governors—state legislators have the greatest influence on both public and private higher education. State legislators appropriate money for everything from scholarships to research. They also make laws that affect all campuses in all sorts of intended and unintended ways. These laws include labor laws, health regulations, economic incentive programs, criminal justice and police laws, gun laws, state employee retirement rules, building code changes, and environmental laws. The list is almost endless. Typically, citizens of a state mostly care about enacted laws that are well publicized and may affect them directly, such as a tax increase. But university government relations officers have to slog through hundreds if not thousands of proposed law and rule changes that might affect the complex institution that we call a university. If even one of these proposed laws might actually be passed, it is best to know what motivates and influences a legislator.

Our Opinion: Make Higher Education Affordable
for Everyone

—July 10, 2008, editorial in the *Times-Reporter*
(Dover-New Philadelphia, Ohio)

Here is a true story about affordability.

My office phone rang late on a summer Friday afternoon. Not many people were around. The young man on the other end of the line identified himself as Paul, an employee in the office of a state lawmaker representing a city on the other side of the state. Paul said that his boss would like to talk to me about an issue at my university. Apparently, a constituent had complained that the room and board costs were doubling. She doubted that she could afford to keep her son at the university if that was indeed the case. Concerned, and wanting to know whether the rise in costs was true, the state representative requested a return call immediately. I wrote down the representative's cell phone number and promised Paul I would call.

Doubling our room and board costs? Unaware of dramatic changes in tuition and fees, I doubted that they could be increasing by that amount. But to be honest, I was not sure. Still, I did not know even who had the authority to set room and board rates, so I decided to call the vice president for student affairs, whom I know well. She was at her desk, and she was able to answer my questions. I was relieved to hear that we were increasing our room and board rates just three to six percent, depending on what residence hall the student was in (air conditioning was the determining factor) and what meal plan the student chose. The vice president sent an assistant down to my office with a detailed account of room and board increases for our sister state universities and all the universities in our athletic conference. My university sat comfortably in the middle range.

Armed with this information, I called the state representative without delay. As it happened, I caught him in his car on the way to a funeral home to be with the family of a soldier who had died in Iraq. It was a sudden and sobering reminder that an elected official's duties are not all fun and games. I explained that the room and board increase was only three to six percent, citing the benchmarking statistics. I suggested that perhaps the mother of the student erroneously thought that the yearly cost was only for first semester, which would explain why she assumed the cost had doubled.

The state representative was very pleasant, and glad to learn that we were not doubling our room and board charges. He praised my university and the president, whom he recognized as a state leader in keeping down college costs. But I sensed a tone in his voice, and I knew I had not completely alleviated the issue. "College is just too expensive," he said. "Even with no tuition increase, room and board rates go up, textbooks are expensive, and fuel costs . . . ."

"We can't do much about fuel costs!" I thought, but I kept quiet. Lending a sympathetic ear, I chatted with him until he arrived at the funeral home. He invited me to stop in at his office, since we had never actually met. Nevertheless, he and Paul knew to call me when they needed information. It gave me pause, as we said good-bye, to realize just how much state legislators know about us and how little we know about them—and how dangerous that discrepancy might be. What if, instead of calling me, he had called a press conference, or had railed about us in his party caucus? Then we might have had a big problem on our hands.

Higher Education Cuts Impact Nevada State College

—February, 2008, the *Scorpion's Tale* (Nevada
State College student newspaper)

At the core of the above story, as well as the above headline, is money, of course. The state representative was legitimately concerned about the possibility of my university ripping off one of his constituents. But the representative was also thinking about the state budget, and what could be done to keep universities affordable for state residents. In Ohio, approximately eleven percent of the most recent state budget was devoted to funding higher education. Medicaid match and funding for primary and secondary education are the only areas that receive greater funding than higher education.

Crafting the state budget is the single most important part of a state legislator's job. In fact, the passage of the budget is literally the only responsibility of the legislators. All else follows. It should be noted that twenty-three states use a two-year budget cycle, rather than a cycle of just one year. But a two-year cycle does not necessarily mean that the various appropriations are equal in both years. Beyond Medicaid and education, states are involved in the oversight and operation of a variety of other public activities, such as the National Guard, road construction, state parks, social services, and mental health facilities, to name just a few. But whatever else might be in a law, it all comes down to funding so that the law can be enacted.

Public higher education receives direct state funding for the following purposes:

1. Student subsidy. Administered on the basis of a formula derived from raw student numbers or full-time equivalent numbers, or some combination of both, student subsidies include money for instruction.
2. Scholarship funding. Scholarships go directly to students who are state residents.
3. Research funding. Usually given more for economic development than for pure research, this type of state funding supports "system-wide" projects such as information technology.
4. Capital funding. Construction or renovation of campus buildings is supported by capital funding.
5. Line item funding. Relatively small at the state level, line item funding is essentially the equivalent of congressional earmarks aimed at individual campus projects.

In the abstract, state legislators enjoy funding higher education, despite the popular belief on campuses that the state abhors giving money to universities. Let's analyze for a moment the five categories of funding listed above. Because scholarship money goes directly to constituents, there is nothing for legislators to dislike about it. Research funding is

Mandate Hell

Generally, states are much better—although not masterful—at avoiding unfunded mandates. Congress loves unfunded mandates, and secretly loves imposing them on states. In addition, states generally have balanced budgets. The federal government, though, can run deficits, since it prints our money, as evidenced by the economic stimulus legislation. Is that an oversimplification? No, not really.

---

generally a small pot of money and often produces very tangible results that make for good photo opportunities. Capital funding leads to construction projects that create jobs, many of them union. Line item fundings (if permitted by a state) usually constitute a very small amount of money all-told. Still, lawmakers are happy when they can deliver the projects to their home institutions.

Student subsidy funding, however, is a more complicated issue, both for the legislators and for higher education administrators. Student subsidies are simply money for instruction. Instruction funding pays salaries and supports the cost of operating the academic side of a campus. It is not supposed to go to athletics, buildings, or student services. Student subsidy funding is meant solely for teaching.

Ironically, even though student subsidy is the largest of the five pots of money listed above, it is the one that enjoys the least accountability. Scholarships can be measured by the number of students receiving them and using them to attend the university. State research funding can be measured by the number of start-up companies created. Capital funding builds buildings that legislators can point at, walk through, and take credit for constructing. Line item funding goes to very specific projects with discernible outcomes. But subsidy money is harder to measure. Are faculty members doing a good job teaching? Are students actually learning what they are being taught? Are they being tested? Are classes small enough for effective learning? Are the top professors teaching, or are they performing research?

For decades, governors and legislators grumbled about accountability in teaching, but seldom did these grumblings amount to much. In recent years, spurred on by a variety of reasons, including the economy, globalization, steadily rising tuition, and more vocal parents/constituents, elected officials are demanding—and legislating—that university presidents be assigned more accountability when it comes to state funding. In Ohio, the chancellor of the university system in his new strategic plan states: "All universities will join the national Voluntary System of Accountability, making data available regarding price, financial aid, degree programs, retention and graduation rates, campus safety, student satisfaction, and student learning outcomes." In other words, the state needs to know what it's getting for every tax dollar spent.

Fish to Prof: Stick to Teaching

—July 1, 2008, *Inside Higher Ed*

In an interview on the Web site *Inside Higher Ed* about his new book *Save the World on Your Own Time,* Stanley Fish makes the rather extraordinary claim that an aggressive approach is the best way to handle legislators. He says, "If you embarrass people [legislators] . . . if you make them afraid of you, you are in a better position than you are if you go to them on your knees." I cannot help wondering what my president would say if I told him I was going to adopt a take-no-prisoners approach toward the legislators who approve approximately $110 million in annual funding for my university. I am sure that Mr. Fish is making the point that we do not tell legislators what they ought to do about most legislation and they should not tell us how to teach eighteenth-century French poetry. (I'm not sure we want legislators to know that we do teach eighteenth-century French poetry. I am certain they would tell us what to do with it. *Mon Dieu!*)

I think Mr. Fish—who writes a lively and interesting column online for the *New York Times*—has succumbed to the malady that affects quite a few academics, including most presidents. Some administrators and faculty members believe that legislators are not very smart. They may feel that legislators know little about higher education and its needs. Mr. Fish's bullying strategy supposes that legislators aren't capable of doing what's best for higher education.

This supposition is not only inaccurate, but borders on being dangerous. For example, in an article in the March 27, 2009, issue of the *Chronicle of Higher Education* about the funding battle between The University of Arizona and the Arizona legislature, there were charges from the higher education community that legislators were not educated enough to make decisions on higher education appropriations. In response (on p. 22), "Rep. Vic Williams, a Republican who lists a GED and 'some college' in his biography, said the question of whether lawmakers without four-year degrees were biased against universities was 'inappropriate' and 'inflammatory.'" Calling into question the intelligence of legislators, who hold the purse strings of state governments, is risky, as doing so may (and often does) result in negative consequences for higher education.

The vast majority of legislators are smart men and women. In an unscientific survey of legislative profiles on the Web, approximately 50 percent of U.S. legislators were found to have college degrees. Of the half of the legislators who have degrees, about 20 percent have law degrees. Although not an infallible measure of intelligence, a college degree is a benchmark of education. I imagine that an average university administrator or professor would erroneously guess that the number of well-educated legislators is even lower.

But there is a more important point to understand than whether or not a legislator is educated. It does not matter whether a legislator is as smart as Stanley Fish and reads eighteenth-century French poetry. What matters is whether the legislator supports higher education. There is no way to know how a legislator really feels about higher education until after she is elected for the first time and receives her committee assignments. Before an election, a legislative candidate might come to the university president and declare that he completely supports increased education funding, as well as decreased oversight for higher education. (The perfect candidate!) But because of seniority and party needs (e.g., filling a vacancy on the Health and Human Services Committee), the new legislator may end up with practically no influence on higher education. At the same time, a new legislator from the other party, and from the other side of the state, with no large university in her district may end up with a key seat on the Education Committee. It becomes questionable whether the "perfect candidate" can still influence higher education policy, such as during a party caucus.

There is also much to be said for geography. Legislators from districts with large universities are rarely opposed to supporting higher education. But to repeat what I wrote at the outset of this chapter, even for your closest legislative friend, the university's wishes will come in third behind political self-preservation and party politics. Home legislators *should* be counted on to support the home university. But a good relationship can go sour if the university president appears arrogant and superior to the legislator, or the legislator has a conflict with the board of trustees, or if the distribution of football tickets gets screwed up. A good government relations officer should be able to keep a president and an athletic department in line. But the board of trustees is another matter.

Every institution of higher education, public or private, small or large, has problems with its board and its politics. If you do not think this is true at your institution, then you are too naïve to be in government relations, or you are not in deep enough with the board to know what is going on behind the scenes. Public university boards are often relatively small (under twenty members). They are appointed by the governor or sometimes elected, and often come from the university's immediate geographical area. Community college boards tend to be very localized, whereas state universities might draw members from throughout the state and even from beyond state lines. Private university boards are often large and self-appointing (with a good deal of input from the alumni and development offices), and tend to be more national in scope.

For public universities, in the abstract, it is the legislators and the governor who fund the university while the board oversees how the university is managed. This is the real utopia that Sir Thomas More was writing about before the King chopped off his head. (Tom wanted to be a trustee at Oxford, but Henry had another candidate in mind.) We may have done away with hiring French executioners to stop by the university, but bitter political infighting about board appointments is still very common. Many players weigh in on board appointments: the university president, sitting trustees, the local newspaper(s), the minority community, and the political parties are just the more prominent interest groups. Usually, the faculty and students are clueless that this is going on.

The successful new board appointee usually is a prominent or well-known member of one of the political parties. This immediately sets the

My Professor, My Trustee

Some administrators reading the words above might be upset or even outraged. But after decades of watching and worrying about Board appointments at various universities, I have never seen much faculty/student involvement. Faculty sometimes want a faculty member appointed to a board committee. I have often wondered why faculty do not campaign to the governor for a real appointment. Perhaps some states would prohibit this by law. But I know my state does not. (I hope I have not given away a secret.)

---

board member apart from about half the legislators, and it can happen that if a governor has been in office for a while and makes board appointments, the whole board can come to consist of members of just one political party. This situation can cause real political headaches for the university president. For example, what to do if your university district legislators are from the opposing party? Board members know full well that the trend in state government is to assert more legislative control in the running as well as the funding of universities. Boards are fighting this trend tooth and nail, and university administrations are often caught in the cross fire between their bosses on the board and their bosses in government.

For private universities, in the abstract, the issue is different, as I will discuss in chapter 8. In brief, private universities are partially hamstrung in state (and, for that matter, local) political affairs because many of their board members are from out of state and do not care much about internal state politics. They appropriately see their university as a great place, just as public board members see their university as a great place. The difference is that private university board members do not usually see their university as integrated with its city/town location or its state. It is hard for a board member who is a corporate executive in New York City to get worked up about local issues when he travels to his alma mater only twice a year for board meetings that consist more of good fellowship than tough business decisions. And the board member may be predisposed to assuming that his university is benefiting the community and state just by being there, and should not be subject to bothersome laws and regulations. This prevalent type of attitude obviously annoys elected officials.

Many presidents at both public and private universities correctly believe that they must be the main representative to their boards of trustees. It is arguably the most important role for the president to serve, both in terms of her own preservation and for the fulfillment of the institution's mission and goals. Government relations, though, is just one of a number of increasingly difficult issues affecting trustees. For example, financial management and integrity in today's world are major concerns for trustees. But just as a president must depend on having a smart and honest vice president of finance, he must also depend on having a smart and honest government relations officer to manage the politics of the board.

Higher education leaders visit lawmakers to
protest proposed budget cuts; cite devastating
consequences for California

—April 28, 2008, press release from
The California State University

The following is the first paragraph from the press release cited above:

> Citing the potential for serious harm to the state's economy and future, the leaders of California's three segments of public higher education—the California Community Colleges, the California State University and the University of California—today (Apr. 28) are making a rare joint visit to the state Capitol to urge policymakers to resist deep budgets cuts for public higher education.

A discussion of state government cannot be complete without a discussion of when to drop the polite smile, take the gloves off, and appeal directly to the people for increasing funding for higher education. Stanley Fish proposes talking tough to legislators, which I doubt is ever a good idea. Issuing a statewide, high-profile press release can also work against the government relations officer. Take California, for example. Facing a major budget crisis and substantial cuts to higher education, the three

California university systems on April 28 issued a press release aimed at capturing the hearts and minds of the citizens of the state:

> For the past few months, leaders and other members of the three systems have been engaged in a first-ever joint public education campaign aimed at helping the public and policymakers understand how important the state's investment in public higher education is to California's economy, and to Californians' short- and long-term well being.

From a government relations officer's point of view, this is a disaster. Internally, the communications people have trumped the government relations staff. This no doubt came about because of the frustration of the academic leaders of the institution. I am certain the presidents and provosts said something along the lines of "We've been patient and tried it your way for years, now we're going public" to their government relations people, whether they are university employees or Sacramento lobbyists.

Maybe it had come to this peak of frustration in California. Maybe it was a last-gasp effort. Maybe someone had the quixotic yet ill-considered idea that the public would rise up to advocate for higher education. But this effort simply insults the legislators. They know that an educated populace is better for the economy and for tax revenues than an uneducated populace would be. As I have already pointed out, legislators are not dummies. So now top university officials are going to lecture them about the importance of higher education, while at the same time sending out a press release to rally the electorate to send letters and make phone calls to badger legislators. To demonstrate how important this all is, higher education is making a "rare joint visit." How did the California public interpret that remark? Does the use of the word "rare" mean that higher education usually does not cooperate? Or does it mean that the leaders of higher education are so important (!) that they can only deem it time to get together when there is a genuine crisis. (*We really can't be bothered with you state legislators. But now that you've really screwed up, we're going to get together and straighten you out. And just to rough you up a little, we're going to tell the public we're doing it.*)

Perhaps this strategy worked in California. It is the Eureka state, and maybe the legislators and public yelled "Eureka!" when they read the press release. But I doubt that it did any good, either with government officials or with the public. And quite frankly, I imagine the government relations officers of the university system had to go to the legislators hat in hand after April 28 and attempt to clean up the mess.

Virginia explores ways to keep college affordable

—April 26, 2008, issue of the *Richmond Times-Dispatch*

Stuart Connock is the executive assistant to the president for state governmental relations at the University of Virginia. In 2007 Connock was awarded the Marvin D. "Swede" Johnson Achievement Award, which honors "those who have primary responsibility for state relations at their institution." The award is given annually at the Higher Education Government Relations Conference and is sponsored jointly by the American Association of Community Colleges, the American Association of State Colleges and Universities, the Council for Advancement and Support of Education, and the Association of Public and Land-Grant Universities.

During a pleasant phone conversation, I asked Mr. Connock how he got into university government relations. With a finance background and a University of Virginia (UVa) degree, and having worked for four different Virginia governors on state finances, he had always been close to UVa and admitted having a hand in making sure the university got its fair share of higher education funding over the years. He knew the current UVa president, and he eventually became the university's first full-time government relations officer. He now has an assistant and a secretary, as well.

"I'm the eyes and ears of the president in Richmond," Mr. Connock said. "We track 600 pieces of legislation, and the president gets reports on legislative matters twice a week."

Mr. Connock does not have to register as a state lobbyist. Virginia law has a special "liaison" category and publishes the names of all liaisons. He said that he won the national achievement award because of his efforts in helping to reshape the structure of higher education in Virginia. The new structure was achieved partly in response to state legislators' concerns that higher education was not doing enough to help K–12 education, promote economic development, and facilitate transfers by students between institutions.

I have highlighted Mr. Connock because he is good at his job, and because he has won an award on the strength of his work in university government relations. (Frankly, there are not a lot of awards given out for university government relations work. It's hard to get noticed when your goal in life is generally to stay under the radar.) In addition to having been honored by his award, Mr. Connock is an example of the dogged devotion that is necessary to monitor state government. Mr. Connock does not worry a lot about local Charlottesville politics, and he does not even know the name of the university system's Washington lobbyist. He is totally focused on the 139 Virginia state legislators and the state's executive branch and agencies.

Without admitting that he is suspicious, Mr. Connock knows that any legislator can insert, into any bill, language that can be detrimental to his university. He also recognizes that his flagship university has an obligation to be on guard in protecting all of the state's higher education institutions. Relations between the state and the institutions are usually positive, of course, but at any moment higher education can find itself ensnared by a new law or a new misunderstanding. It is up to Mr. Connock and his higher education colleagues across the country to be on guard.

CHAPTER FIVE

Enslave

The Federal Government

A government relations officer with business in Washington has a lot in common with a criminal under house arrest. (I have always thought the concept of house arrest was strange—confined to your home, you are free to mow the lawn, watch a ballgame on TV, have a glass of wine, and grill a steak. Sounds almost like a typical weekend at my house!) We government relations officers, under our own form of house arrest, are free to move around Washington. We can watch Congress in session, go to a Nationals baseball game, and enjoy great food and beverages. But seldom do we get to do the fun stuff and accomplish very much of significance. That's because we are being controlled and manipulated by powerful forces—namely our congressional delegations and their staffers, as well as federal departments and agencies. Everyone tolerates us when we visit, but our accomplishments are only what those who live and work in Washington want us to accomplish.

Returning to our home university, we attach a report of our Washington accomplishments to our rather hefty expense sheet. The report begins with a highlight. (A highlight is generally defined as actually speaking in person to an *elected* official—Any elected official, even if he or she is not from our state.) Then we move on to list the staffers whom we encountered because "these are the people who can really get things done." Then we regurgitate the discussion from a meeting with a couple of lowly officials from some education association. (This is somewhat ironic, because while we are listing them on our report to our boss they are listing us on their report to their boss.) Finally, we touch base with our lobbying contacts, who we hope have at least one tangible piece of good news that we can carry home in triumph.

Whew! What a trip.

The problem with the federal government is that we do not understand it. Oh, government relations officers understand Washington better than anyone else at their university, but that is not saying much. The federal government is so large and so complex that it defies reason and comprehension. It is also overwhelmed by input. It absorbs all information like a gigantic sponge crafted in marble. Still, it is a nice place to visit. We just have to figure out what we are doing there.

At the state level, a university—even a private university—can have great influence. From funding to enacting laws, higher education affects the lives of just about everyone, from the governor to agency heads to first-term legislators. But at the federal level, a university has little influence. That is why it must reorient its thinking and its goals. A university needs to move just an inch at the federal level to reap huge benefits. A million dollars is insignificant to the federal budget, but a million-dollar earmark is a huge sum and a tremendous accomplishment to a small university. Changing just one sentence in federal legislation might go unnoticed, but that one sentence could affect a campus for years. Figuring out how to get the most out of small legislative changes then becomes the raison d'être of the government relations officer working in Washington.

Every government relations officer has just three established contacts in Washington to whom she is obliged to pay some attention. The three contacts include exactly one congressperson and two U.S. senators. Of course, a congressperson is much more interested in your university than a senator would be unless you are very lucky and the senator is an alum. (It does happen. A senator has to be an alum of someplace!) But senators are very busy people dealing with very important national issues. And, of course, there are only a hundred of them doing all the work. So, your local congressperson—who is one of 435—ends up being your most important contact in Washington.

My congressperson lives in the Rayburn Building, which was opened in 1965 and is named after Sam Rayburn, the Texas Democrat and Speaker of the House who served in Congress for 48 years. The Capitol Architect's Web site neatly summarizes how the Rayburn building was created: "In

Political Tour Stop #1

Reagan National Airport (previously Washington National) opened in June 1941 on land originally owned (way back) by descendants of George Washington. There may be no airport anywhere more convenient to its city's downtown than Reagan. But that convenience comes at a price. Except for coming in over water to short runways in San Francisco and LaGuardia, landing and taking off at Reagan is really, really frightening.

March 1955 Speaker Sam Rayburn introduced an amendment for a third House office building, although no site had been identified, no architectural study had been done, and no plans prepared" (www.aoc.gov/cc/cobs/rhob.cfm). No wonder that it took ten years to get the building constructed. Coincidentally, our congressperson did the same thing for our campus 50 years later, announcing that she had arranged for a federal agency to build a large research building on our campus "although no site had been identified, no architectural study had been done, and no plans prepared." Do not get me wrong. We were happy to get the building, but its gestation demonstrates how little actual control we have over Congress and its members.

A small private university on the other side of my state created an institute named after its congressperson. Each year the administration and faculty there had a luncheon and gave out a couple of scholarships in the name of this congressperson, who always spoke at the event and effusively praised the university, especially the institution's decidedly conservative bent. The university was rewarded with a steady stream of funding from the federal government. Establishing an institute is a viable and oft-practiced strategy of interacting with a congressperson, and possibly benefiting from that engagement. But be certain the congressperson is a lifer from a safe district. Do not delude yourself that the other political party is not watching your support of the incumbent and will not take revenge in the future if ever given the chance. (This actually happened to the private university mentioned above, when the veteran congressperson rather abruptly retired and a member of the other political party took his place.)

The importance of a congressperson is measured by which commit-tees he or she serves on. Committees are the heart of government on the House side of Congress, whereas the full Senate is the heart of govern-ment on the Senate side. (This is a bit of an overstatement, but does con-tain a basic constitutional truth.) Committee assignments, therefore, can make or break a congressperson's career. Serving as a committee chair is often the ultimate goal of a congressperson, not only because of the con-trol over a committee that the chair has, but also because of the party influence the chair person wields. If a chair's party controls the House, being a committee chair means that the congressperson is part of the House leadership.

Sometimes, however, being merely a member of a more important committee is preferable to being a chair on a less influential one. Just this year, my university's congressperson relinquished a chair of a lesser com-mittee to become a member of what is arguably one of the two most powerful committees in the entire House. But beyond being a chair of a committee or a member of a powerful committee, it is even more impor-tant to chair a subcommittee that appropriates money. Then, the con-gressperson becomes a "Cardinal," as David Keene explains in an article on the Web site *The Hill:* "Anyone who knows much about real power in Congress knows that almost every member of the House and Senate lusts after a seat on the Appropriations Committee and hopes one day to achieve the status of Cardinal. The Cardinals, of course, are the folks who chair the various Appropriations Committee subcommittees and literally control the billions of dollars that pass through their hands" (thehill.com/ david-keene/feinsteins-cardinal-shenanigans-2007-04-30.html).

Universities have the greatest difficulty not if their congressperson is out of the money loop, but if the congressperson either is not interested in higher education or is ideology-wise at cross purposes with the general political culture on campus. As I discuss in chapter 4, concerning some state legislators, some congresspersons just do not seem to care much about education and/or higher education. They may have their own per-sonal priorities, or may have had other priorities assigned to them when they first entered Congress. With this type of congressperson, the one advantage a university has is that the congressperson (or more likely a friendly staff member) will at least do what is needed, so that it will not

Political Tour Stop #2

Speaking of cardinals, during the pope's recent trip to the United States, he held mass at the new ballpark of the Washington Nationals, formerly the Montreal Expos. Not the smartest diplomatic move—stealing one of only two Canadian Major League Baseball teams. It would have been wiser to have acquired a team from Cuba. (Anyone remember ping-pong and China?) Anyway, the stadium is beautiful and well worth a visit. It sits next to Washington's other river, the Anacostia, and the ballpark designers have built in vistas of the river and the Naval Yard. And be sure to go by subway, which is quite a trip by itself.

appear that he or she is avoiding the university. Just do not expect any large windfall.

Conversely, a congressperson ideologically at odds with a university can be a big problem. This is especially true if the institution's president cannot reach out to the congressperson by being cordial and diplomatic. Many times the stalemate between congressperson and president is political. The situation is often exacerbated, intentionally or unintentionally, by faculty members. Except for mayors, congresspersons are the highest-profile local politicians. Most intelligent people know their congressperson and his or her party affiliation, and also know if their person is extremely liberal or extremely conservative. If you doubt that, watch your city newspaper(s) letters to the editors for the month, and you will be surprised how often regular citizens comment on your congressperson's political stances. If your university is in the district of a hostile congressperson who takes issue with some liberal institute on campus, or with the value of tenure, the university government relations officer might be the situation's only hope. In this case, backroom conversations with a sympathetic if not completely friendly congressional staffer could be the best way to get anything done. At least the government relations officer can find out what or who irritates the congressperson the most and try to tone down the ongoing rhetoric if possible. A more tricky strategy, one that cannot be pursued without the university president's consent and participation, is to get the congressperson together with select members of the university trustees. They probably know each other anyway, but having the trustees at least mildly defend the university might help mollify the congressperson's mindset.

How does an institution of higher education decide whether sending its government relations officer to Washington is a worthwhile proposition? Will he affect the course of American higher education? Will she bring back congressional promises of significant earmarks for the university? Or, will he only enjoy a good time on the university's nickel? To determine whether a trip to our nation's capital is worthwhile, the university administration might want to follow these guidelines:

- Make certain that one of the many higher education associations in Washington (see chapter 7) is not already handling the situation. That is, after all, what such associations are supposed to be doing. The recent stimulus funding feeding frenzy clearly demonstrates the importance of higher education associations. These associations quickly and effectively conquered the bureaucratic maze the university had had difficulty navigating *just to apply* for funding. The associations especially kept the pressure on federal agencies to address higher education needs, ranging from scientific equipment to infrastructure. If the institution belongs to one or more of these associations, perhaps a phone call is all that is needed to get some help.
- If there is a need for an institution to speak with its representatives or senators, make certain that the politicians will be in Washington, and make (and then confirm) an appointment. Though it is easier and cheaper to see the representative back in his or her home district office, it is okay occasionally to drop into his Washington office. Washington visits are okay, because you will meet or reconnect with staffers who answer phones and deal with legislation, and who almost never visit the home district. But when you meet with your elected official in his or her office, just be sure there is some Washington "angle" that will engage the congressperson or senator.
- For the most part, agency headquarters and directors are located only in Washington. Therefore, if the university is involved in an ongoing issue like a proposal for continued grant funding or for

building a research building on campus, then a trip to the capital to nail down particulars is often necessary and prudent. Again, meeting bureaucrats who shudder at the thought of ever having to leave Washington is the more valuable choice.

- Check up on the university lobbyists. A face-to-face meeting with the lobbyist helps keep your university's agenda as a high priority. Not all universities have their own Washington lobbyists, of course. But no matter how good a lobbyist might be, just showing up in their Washington office gets their attention. At least showing up should be worth a free lunch or dinner, paid for by the lobbyist (and later, of course, billed back to the university).

- Attend a relevant conference or convention. Although Washington has many interesting places to visit, it still does not have an ocean, golf courses, casinos, or Broadway shows. The nation's capital is full of intelligent and powerful people who are willing to cross town— but not the country—to speak and advise. Washington conferences, with their particular emphasis on how to get things done and accomplish goals, can be very helpful to the government relations officer's career. And "free time" at a conference in Washington also means that planners have thoughtfully set aside time for Hill visits, where university officials can meet with congressional representatives about issues important to their institutions. Hill visits may not be nearly as much fun as a round of golf, but they can be of tremendous value while in Washington.

- Testify before Congress, or serve on a prestigious academic panel. Although these are usually fool's errands, since they have little, if any, profound influence on policy or lawmaking, congressional testimony and panel discussions certainly are ego-boosting if the testifier is your president or institution's leading researcher. And the appearance will most likely garner wide and positive media coverage back home.

All these are valid reasons to spend the money and make the effort to go to Washington. Quite frankly, more may come of any one of the above reasons than usually comes from most other university-paid trips around the country.

Political Tour Stop #3

Visit the Thomas Jefferson Memorial in West Potomac Park. You can see it fairly close at hand in the cab coming from or going to the airport, but take a walk to the open-air portico and dome covering the imposing statue of the president. It is significant that Jefferson overlooks Washington. It seems that the site of our nation's capital was chosen one evening when Jefferson asked James Madison and Alexander Hamilton to dinner. Honoring a need to appease the southern states—a process that continues to this day—these founding fathers of our nation, so wise in so many other ways, decided to buy swampland. Incidentally, George—our first president—was embarrassed that the new city was named after him, and he referred to the place as Federal City. The name hung around for most of the first half of the nineteenth century, until "Washington" became commonly used.

Since World War II, most states have been apportioning funds for general operations to higher education with few strings attached. In contrast, the federal government typically funds specific higher education programs with many strings attached. As noted in chapter 4, states are increasingly asking for accountability in higher education, and are increasingly targeting funds for specific programs, especially in applied research. At the state level, this has evolved partially because state legislators have noticed that federal funding seems to get more attention from universities than state funding does, even though, in the aggregate, state funding is much greater.

The federal government funds higher education primarily through three channels: (1) massive scholarship and loan programs, (2) research funding through government departments and agencies such as the Department of Defense (DoD) and the National Institutes of Health (NIH), and (3) directed funding (called earmarks) that is usually designated for a particular institution. Generally, these three categories work well together, since they are targeted for three different purposes. Scholarships and loans help students attend college. Research funding promotes new knowledge and the welfare of the nation. Earmarks often construct buildings, and ideally fill particular voids that are missed by other private, state, or federal funding.

Except for Hillsdale, a private college in Michigan, all institutions of higher education today receive federal funds. (Here are my questions for Hillsdale: What would you do if the state government funded a sewer project for the city of Hillsdale that included the college? Would you look the other way? Would you pay for the college's portion of the sewer? Would you put in your own septic tanks?) For small universities and colleges, both private and public, as well as for community colleges, most of this federal funding is for scholarships and loans. The larger the school, the more research funding and earmarks it receives. Yet even a tiny school, if it has the good fortune of being the only institution of higher learning in a congressperson's district, might receive an earmark or two.

An earmark or a congressionally directed appropriation consists of language within a federal bill, or even just a committee report that provides funding to nonfederal entities (often higher education) without going through the normal legislative process or a competitive grant process. It should be noted that more than a few university administrators over the years have spoken out against earmarks. The *Yale Daily News* from March 26, 2008, reported that Yale receives no earmarks. Yale University president Richard Levin is quoted as saying, "It's the wrong way to allocate funds to the universities. It should be to the maximum extent possible, all by competition with peer review." The article pointed out, however, that only one other Ivy League university, Princeton, did not receive any earmarks. Besides sometimes being philosophically opposed to the concept of "no competition," as stated by President Levin, another criticism of earmarks has been that awards sometimes go to universities that may not even have programs in certain research areas, or that lack the critical mass needed to use the money wisely. Conversely, administrators do not like to be stuck with making up the funding shortfall when an earmark is insufficient to complete a project or a building.

Nevertheless, for the vast majority of government relations officers, earmarks are the only Washington funding that is really in play. Scholarship funding such as Federal Pell Grants goes directly to the student. Major research funding coming out of the NIH or DoD is processed through bureaucrats and often subject to peer review. Earmarks, in any case, consisting of about 5 percent of all federal research spending, are doled out at the discretion of members of Congress. ("Ay, there's the rub," as Hamlet famously said.)

Of course, earmarks are not just for institutions of higher education. Over the years, Senator Robert Byrd has practically rebuilt the entire state of West Virginia using earmarks. Many local and state governmental units lobby for and receive earmarks. Many earmarks fulfill legitimate needs, but occasionally they fund questionable projects, which are the kinds of recipients that make the headlines. An example of a questionable project was the "Bridge to Nowhere" in Alaska, which after pressure and ridicule resulted in a moratorium on congressional earmarks. (Well, not exactly a moratorium . . . .)

Not in the history of the Ringling Bros. Circus has one done more contorting than Congress over a three-year period to sort of end but kind of put restrictions on earmarks, but not really (if you see what I mean). The process of doing so was ugly, but also fascinating. For a while, federal agencies were empowered to distribute a certain type of earmark. But agencies (as agencies normally do) tended to hold onto the money, much to the frustration of recipients and Congress alike. Half-finished projects, whether for construction or research, ended up in a weird congressional twilight zone. Washington lobbyists, paid by universities for one purpose—acquiring earmarks—were on high alert but essentially paralyzed while their connection to earmarks was under press scrutiny. Government relations officers on campus wearily explained, over and over again, that researchers, provosts, and presidents just had to be patient and this too will pass. Which it did, albeit with stricter restrictions and lobbying reforms.

So, as David Letterman might say: "How can I get me one of them earmarks?"

Well, the very best way to snag an earmark is to hire an extremely high-profile Washington lobbying firm and pay the firm at least $100,000 annually and wait two years. If that plan will not fly with your board of trustees, try the following:

- Decide who will be in charge of obtaining the earmark: the president, the provost, the vice president for research, or, if you have one, the government relations officer. This person will be in charge of the project from beginning to end.

- Establish campus guidelines for earmarks. The Office of Research Development at Eastern Michigan University uses an eight-point checklist for successful earmark projects:

  1. Earmarks must serve "a national or regional need."
  2. The university must ensure that it has the "infrastructure and capacity to sustain" the funds.
  3. Any earmarks sought must align with the university's strategic plan.
  4. The funds must have the support of Congress and any affiliated federal agencies.
  5. Earmarks must not be part "of any competitive bidding structure."
  6. Budgets must be realistic and reasonable.
  7. Researchers receiving federal earmarks must "have experience in the topic."
  8. Proposals for earmarks must be "well written and comprehensive."

  From fiscal year 2003 through 2007, Eastern Michigan received ten earmarks worth a total of $9.9 million; see www.ord.emich.edu/funding/special_opp/fed_earmarks.html.

- Decide if you will approach your congressperson or senators to carry the water. The normal choice will be your university's congressperson, because he and his staff are accessible. In contrast with a busy senator, your congressperson will have a reasonable number of requests, and will probably have some knowledge of your university, and so will be able to defend the request. But a U.S. senator might be a more reasonable choice if she is an alum, or if your university is the largest in your state. But this is important: inform the other two what you are doing. You will eventually need their support.

- Decide on one or two reasonable projects that can be represented by researchers who clean up well enough for a trip to Washington. Projects do not always have to be scientific in nature, but scientific research receives most of the big-money awards. An earmark for the arts, humanities, or social sciences might be for a decent amount of money, and will get some street cred back on campus. Create a classy spiral-bound notebook describing your school, the project(s), and the researchers in some—but not too much—detail. Do not create a Power Point presentation and expect politicians to watch it.

- Determine a strategic time to visit Washington to lobby for your earmark, and decide who is going along. It is best that the president go, as well as the chief researcher/author of the project.
- Remember that humility is always preferable to arrogance.
- Understand that you will not be mad if you get turned down the first year. Believe me, you will probably do all right the second year. Or, maybe the third year.
- When you do receive an award, offer profuse thanks to the elected officials involved, especially to their staff members. At a former institution where I worked, we actually named the lab we received funding for after our congressperson. Why not?

Stephen Joel Trachtenberg, the recently retired president of George Washington University (GWU), has written a memoir entitled *Big Man on Campus* (Simon & Schuster, 2008). It is an engaging look back at his years as president, first of the University of Hartford and then of GWU. Trachtenberg has a fair amount to say about the federal government, since GWU is physically just about the closest higher education institution to the Capitol. He writes, "In my judgment, Congress's interest in higher education will continue to increase and senators will keep watching what is happening on our campuses" (page 6). He immediately cites the congressional issue du jour at mid-decade—the growth of huge endowments at major universities. This issue made for good newspaper copy around the country, and caused consternation in university offices of development. The standard way the universities resolved this issue was to announce new scholarship programs to "give back" money to students. Who can be against scholarships? Still, the fact of the matter was that this issue never engendered much concern back at Ordinary State University, because the vast majority of schools do not have huge endowments. In

Political Tour Stop #4

George Washington University is a fine school among many fine schools in the city. It is located not far from the White House, adjacent to Washington Circle. Its campus is not particularly picturesque, although it does have the distinction of being one of the most expensive schools in the country. In 2008, GWU received two congressional earmarks, one for health-professional training for students from D.C. and one for the Eleanor Roosevelt Papers Project. The two earmarks totaled $666,155. The sponsors included Senator Hatch from Utah, Congressman Moran from Virginia, and Delegate Norton from the District.

any case, during the recession every university was concerned about having any endowment left.

Nevertheless, the point Dr. Trachtenberg is making is germane. Higher education is under increasing scrutiny from the federal government. A subsequent legislative issue, following congressional unhappiness with excessive university endowments, has been the ongoing student loan scandal, which did affect practically every institution of higher education. Bank lenders over the years had been making arrangements with schools and their financial officers to create essentially noncompetitive student loans. Congressional action, besides outrage, included House passage of the 2007 Student Loan Sunshine Act, which was never passed by the Senate into law. The Obama administration recently has proposed to end bank-based student lending altogether.

The loan scandal was a particularly thorny issue for government relations officers at universities because it involved an area of expertise that few government relations officers knew much about. Most of us hurriedly educated ourselves about financial aid and loans and sweetheart deals. ("Please, God, not at my university!") But the issue highlights the most difficult and frustrating aspect of the profession of government relations— you must know about everything going on at your school, and you must know enough to advise the president at a moment's notice.

Bloated endowments and the student loan scandal are examples of how the federal government enslaves higher education. Even prestigious Ivy League universities, with huge endowments and alumni representation in Congress, quickly caved to pressure, fearful of legislation that might harm fund-raising or threaten their savings, such as requiring a minimal 5 percent spending requirement per year. The mammoth Higher Education Reauthorization Act that lumbered slowly through Congress was filled with other issues that were difficult to sort out, such as how they would affect individual campuses, either fiscally or musically. Yes, I said musically. Congress was heavily lobbied by sectors of the music industry to force universities to police students from illegally downloading music without paying for it. There was even a list of universities that had the most student violators. I know this because the university where I received my graduate degrees showed up on the list. (Back then, of course, we were listening to music on vinyl records.)

But the issue that created the most consternation around the nation was Department of Education Secretary Margaret Spelling's proposal to link federal funding to universities with accreditation outcomes, to ensure quality education. This proposal got the attention of everyone at universities without their government relations officers having to cry wolf in empty hallways. Since then the proposal has been modified, but it is not going away.

Like New York and Los Angeles, Washington is a popular setting for books and movies. Most political junkies love the melodramas set against the background of the federal government. I am a devoted reader of Vince Flynn's political thrillers, often set in Washington. My favorite films about presidents are *The American President* and *Dave*. My favorite television presidents are Geena Davis in *Commander-in-Chief* and Martin Sheen in *The West Wing*. Of course, the most influential of these fictional depictions of the city and the president was the long-running *West Wing*. Once, while I was making a call on a White House staffer in the Executive Office Building, she said I should stop down at the Indian Treaty Room, an ornate ceremonial reception and meeting room that actually looks down on the West Wing of the White House. I found myself more fascinated by staring down at the roof of the West Wing than I was by the history of the Indian Treaty Room.

Political Tour Stop #5

Well, it's time to go home. So, for a last adventure in our nation's capital, I would suggest walking, not riding the elevator, up all 897 steps of the Washington Monument and gazing out over the city from the pyramidion. This offers a sobering but enlightening view of the complexity and size of our Federal City, and on a clear day, you might see your own university.

What was interesting about *The West Wing* was that it often dealt with the White House negotiating with Congress over real issues. It portrayed in occasionally undecipherable dialogue the complicated interplay between White House officials and members of Congress and their staffers. Originally, the series was going to be simply about the men and women who worked in the West Wing, with the president intended as a peripheral character. But Martin Sheen's intriguing characterization of Jed Bartlet, former governor of Vermont now president, became more central to the plot. He also became the president we all wanted in real life.

Of course, that is unfair to George Bush, Bill Clinton, and Barack Obama. The show actually began in the fall of 1999, near the end of the Clinton administration. Fictional portrayals of Washington and national politics are just that—fiction. For example, *The West Wing* ended with the election to the presidency of an obscure Hispanic congressman from Texas. (An unknown minority member of Congress actually becoming president! How could such a thing ever happen?)

CHAPTER SIX

No Such Thing as a Free Lunch

Lobbyists Today

First, a basic definition of federal lobbyists.

Lobbying, at a university, is the hiring of individuals or businesses—often law firms—to work with university officials, including faculty members, the president, government relations officers, and research administrators, to obtain government funding, and to influence government policy. Lobbying has taken place as long as there have been governments. In America, the term "lobbying" dates back to the Civil War era. During the Grant administration, office seekers and men who sought to gain the favor of the president lined up in the lobby of the Willard Hotel, a few blocks from the White House, where the president sat in an easy chair and smoked a cigar after lunch. This same era saw political cartoonists like Thomas Nast portray lobbyists as fat-cat seekers of government favors.

Charles S. Mack, in his well-known book about lobbying entitled *Business, Politics, and the Practice of Government Relations*, lists five reasons that "organizations lobby public officials":

1. To gain benefits or relief unavailable in the private sector.
2. To gain or retain an economic advantage.
3. To gain relief or advantage at one level of government that has been denied at another.
4. To create beneficial programs.
5. To resolve public problems that only governments can handle.

Institutions of higher education are interested almost exclusively in point two, lobbying for extra funding at the federal level. Higher education associations, however, both in Washington and in the state capitals (see chapter 7), tend to focus on point four, creating and maintaining beneficial programs for their member institutions. Lobbyists are a very diverse group. There are tens of thousands of registered lobbyists in Washington (one Web estimate puts the number at nearly 40,000) and tens of thousands more spread across the country. Some are former politicians, and some are former congressional staff members. Many lobbyists are attorneys who have formed their own lobbying group, or work for a lobbying wing of a large law firm. Many lobbyists are professionals who have worked most of their lives for a business or industry and have gotten into lobbying for those businesses or industries. A growing number of lobbyists work for governments or businesses outside the United States who want to influence U.S. policies. Lobbyists tend to specialize in terms of broad topics, such as health care, agriculture, or trade agreements. Some specialize in relationships with politicians and their staffs, whereas others may never see politicians. Some deal only with Republicans. Others deal only with Democrats. Some are money raisers. Others never talk about money.

Lobbyists may have a poor reputation with the public, but Senator Joe Lieberman, in his book *In Praise of Public Life,* describes the importance of a lobbyist's role, which few people realize. He writes:

> Although special interest groups have contributed greatly to the partisanship and frequent gridlock in Congress, as I will soon explain, they can sometimes help a legislator make the system work. If I can convince an interest group to support one of my legislative proposals, that brings with it lobbying support in Congress and letters and phone calls to every senator from the group's members back home, whether they are environmentalists, municipal officials, realtors, a women's group or any other organized association. That naturally helps broaden the support for my proposal. (p. 109)

A Worthy Example

In the summer of 2008, the higher education community was rocked by the extraordinary news that the University of Chicago was establishing a lobbying office in Washington, D.C. Well, perhaps "rocked" and "extraordinary" are both overstatements. First of all, who knew that the university did not already have an office? Second, did anyone care? Nevertheless, the announcement merited a rather lengthy article in the July 17, 2008, edition of *Inside Higher Ed,* which featured the appointment of Scott Sudduth to head the office. The online daily described Sudduth as "a long-time lobbyist who's spent nearly two decades representing universities on Capitol Hill."

The article stated that part of the reason for the new office was the university's management of both the Argonne National Laboratory and the Fermi National Accelerator Laboratory. In addition to maintaining funding for the famous labs, university officials declared that Chicago "wants to help shape public policy on subjects as diverse as health care and student loans, becoming more of an advocate for higher education as a whole."

Near the end of the piece, we are told that "For years, it had been accepted that the powerful Republican House speaker, Rep. Dennis Hastert, would ensure the labs in his home state were taken care of in the budget. But after Hastert resigned in 2007, long-held traditions appeared to dissolve." In fact, the budget for Fermi was promptly cut by $52 million in the 2008 budget. Mr. Sudduth stated that his job (perhaps his real job, instead of advocating for all of higher education) would be "educating Congress on the importance of the labs."

This one story about the University of Chicago neatly sums up some of the questions that arise out of federal lobbying, including:

- Should the university have a permanent presence in Washington?
- To what extent can the university depend on national education organizations to take care of business that affects only it?
- Can *any* lobbyist in Washington help the university, or must the university hire the highest-profile lobbyist around?
- Will the university's trustees, faculty, and students approve of spending a lot of money on a lobbyist to protect funding for a specific project that many of them might not care about? Or, would it be more politically astute to generalize and say that the university is working for the betterment of all of higher education?

- Can the university, rather than hire a lobbyist, find a member of Congress to champion its causes?
- Is it even possible to educate Congress?

The answer to each of these questions is both yes and no. And therein lies the dilemma.

The Ask

The University of Chicago story above illustrates a primary principle about lobbying: identify the ask. Successful lobbyists are always specific in what they ask for. The nature of the project is specific. The amount of money is specific. How the money will be spent is specific. When the project will be completed is specific. Who will benefit from the project is specific.

This seemingly simple concept is surprisingly difficult for many people in higher education to grasp. Trustees, presidents, faculty researchers, and other faculty members have difficulty putting the whole package together. The main problem, which is pervasive throughout all of higher education, is accountability. (*Give us money and we'll make good use of it— state subsidy, alumni gifts, corporate donations, tuition dollars—trust us. We have all sorts of great ideas on how to use it. And the fact is you all don't understand the complexity of universities. Both of us will be much better off if you just let us take care of your money. Oh, and by the way, we can use some more.*)

A *New York Times* article from August 24, 1999, about higher education lobbying for earmarks, quotes Robert Walker, a longtime Pennsylvania congressman who retired in 1997, about an encounter with university representatives. "I asked one [a university president] what he was going to use the money for. He didn't know but said he was sure it would come in handy." (Hint: University presidents and members of Congress are not in the same club!)

Smart lobbyists know that this approach is likely to fail. There has to be accountability. There has to be a demonstration that money will be spent in a specific way for a specific project. One of the misunderstandings about earmarks for the uninitiated is the belief that congressional earmarks are for the university, as in a new building or for research, as in a scientific investigation. Earmarks are not for the glory of the university or the researcher—they are for the glory of the congressperson. Effective lobbyists understand that a congressperson is first promoting vested interests and react to those interests accordingly.

Say your public university, private university, or community college is looking to hire its first ever Washington lobbyist. Your president and government relations officer ask colleagues and perhaps your national association to suggest some appropriate lobbying firms. You get some names, make appointments, and schedule a trip to Washington. The university contingent includes the president, the board chairman, the government relations officer, and the vice president for finance. You have even taken the advice of one colleague and put together a spiral-bound notebook of three earmark ideas: a new science building, an environmentally oriented research project, and a teacher-training idea. You have a lovely time in Washington visiting five very swanky offices. One even overlooks the Capitol itself, with a conference room to die for and bottled water with personalized labels of the firm's name. You return home to make a decision. How do you decide which firm to pick?

Simple. Choose the lobbying firm that catered *least* to your interests. The firms that enthusiastically embraced your three ideas are to be avoided. The firm that politely listened to your pitch and then quietly pushed your notebook off to the side is the one that will be most effective for you. Why? Because that firm knows that even if you have a friendly congressperson, he or she will have an agenda different from your institution's agenda. Ask the lobbying firm to describe your congressperson and your state's senators. If they answer in generalities, they are not for you. But if they can specifically describe the congresspersons' and senators' backgrounds and political agendas, then they can advise you on the development of buildings and projects that will be supported and ultimately funded. A congressperson may be devoted to water pollution cleanup. Your government relations officer should know this, but maybe she does not. Maybe your university does not have any pollution researchers. Then go home and hire one and come back next year with a proposal. Finally, hire the lobbying firm that has figured this out, and have its lobbyists go to work on your behalf.

A Washington lobbying firm will cost an institution of higher education easily more than $100,000 annually. In the January 30, 2009, issue of *Inside Higher Ed*, an article on lobbying reported that "Colleges and other education organizations reported spending more than $100 million on lobbying the federal government in 2008, passing that milestone for the first time, according to the Center for Responsive Politics' Opensecrets.org project." Universities with a lobbying firm in place during the passage of the American Recovery and Reinvestment Act were more than rewarded, because the lobbyists for those firms understood how the Washington bureaucracy works and how stimulus funds are eventually distributed.

Working the Deal

I asked Andy, the primary contact at my university's lobbying firm, to describe the most important aspect of his firm's relationship to my university. Without hesitating, he answered that coordination and cooperation are essential. Strong relationships with campus officials "keep all of us aware of what is going on back at the university." What a coincidence! Andy's concerns are the same as mine, *and I'm on campus most of the time!*

But Andy is right. If a university is going to pay a great deal of money for a lobbying firm, the university has to keep the firm informed about progress being made back on campus. The problem the university has in this regard is that on campus there are lots of people interested in a federal earmark, or some other aspect of federal legislation. And the higher the stakes, the more people, naturally, who are interested. For example, while the government relations officers are working the political angle, the vice president for research and the researchers are working the funding agency angle. The president or board chair meanwhile sees the congressperson at a reception, and they discuss the project's progress. At the same time, the vice president for finance wonders exactly when the funding will show up, to pay for the assistants that the researcher is already hiring. And the communications people want a photo for the press release they plan to issue for some much-needed positive publicity. The provost and dean want to know who will teach the researcher's classes while the researcher is researching the earmark.

Lobbying firms do not have to be informed about every detail of these internal issues. But they do need to know when a campus issue erupts into a problem that could delay or even derail the earmark. What if the researcher decides to take his or her earmark and transfer to another university? Often there is language in contracts and agreements to prevent such an occurrence, but a principal researcher could still abruptly move, say, for personal reasons. The lobbying firm must be constantly in the communication's loop.

Another reason to keep strong ties with Washington is that many earmarks have multi-year implications. This is especially true when a university obtains federal funding for campus construction. Construction projects are so expensive—especially if science laboratories are involved—that one congressional strategy is to spread funding over several years. Another strategy is to commit a federal agency to the construction of a building and then move the line item out of the earmark budget and into the agency's budget. As you might imagine, agencies are not always thrilled when this happens. Your lobbying firm will be absolutely invaluable in sorting through such complicated processes.

State Lobbyists: The Hall of the States

On North Capitol Street in Washington, just a couple of blocks from the Capitol, is an eight-story glass building known as the Hall of the States. The building is managed by the State Services Organization (SSO), which was created in 1976 as "a joint venture of the Council of State Governments, the National Conference of State Legislators, and the National Governors Association" (see sso.org). About two-thirds of the nation's state governments have offices in the Hall of States, and the building also houses the Washington offices of two major television networks (which often film from the roof, using the Capitol as a backdrop).

It may seem strange at first that state governments have to establish what is essentially their own lobbying operations in Washington. After all, isn't that what a state's congressperson(s) and senators are supposed to do? Of course it is, and they do. But federal elected officials do not have much time to worry themselves about all the matters that concern governors and state legislators. Occasionally, there are situations where most of the federal politicians of a state are not of the same political party as the governor and most of the state legislators. This is one reason, among others, that university government relations officers can be found prowling the corridors of the Hall of the States.

Seeing your state government's Washington representative, who in most cases is appointed by the governor, in the Hall of the States, or in some other Washington office, is a little like entering the twilight zone. (As a general rule, college and university representatives travel to Washington to ask for money. They travel to their state capitols to protect money already received or to collect money owed.) Calling on your representative in the Hall of the States signals that you are seeking a state ally, because the university believes the state may have a vested interest in the project. Often, this involves lining up cooperation between or among states. Some examples include joint research earmarks, universities in close proximity, yet across state borders, that want to collaborate on projects, and multi-state efforts like protecting the water resources of the Great Lakes or the Chesapeake Bay. State government representatives not only talk to their state counterparts, but also have a direct line to the governor and the governor's chief of staff.

An Unnecessary Luxury?

As we will see in chapters 10 and 11, on the career aspects of being a government relations officer in higher education, many government relations officers began their careers by lobbying at the state level. This is where real politics happens. Millions of dollars of subsidy, research, and scholarship money are at stake. Yet state politicians, including the governor (if you are persistent), are readily available. Politicians' schedules are widely disseminated, so one can find out at which expensive hotels or cheap motels they stay. It is not hard to discover where they go for drinks and where they eat their dinners. Almost every state capitol has some form of a gauntlet, where state senators or state representatives must walk between two lines of reporters, lobbyists, and ordinary citizens to get to chambers or committee rooms, or even out of the statehouse. Since most states have restored state capitol buildings instead of erecting new ones (Maryland's capitol is 228 years old; Hawaii's is the newest), it is often possible to be very near politicians during session. In the Ohio senate, for example, there is public seating within ten or twelve feet of senators. That close, it is easy to have your presence felt. Therefore, with all of these possibilities of interaction, why should institutions of higher education employ independent state lobbyists in addition to employing federal lobbyists?

The answer to that question centers on why lobbyists are extremely important at all levels of government, but especially important at the state level. That answer simply is information. Lobbyists supply legislators with information, almost all of it factual. Good lobbyists identify their sources, but they also identify their biases. If the legislator has questions, lobbyists are usually the ones to answer them. Remember, state legislators have very small staffs. A state representative in my state who is not in a leadership position has one full-time assistant. A state senator has two. No one individual can be expected to understand all the complexities of insurance legislation, environmental legislation, health legislation, agriculture legislation, and, of course, higher education legislation. Lobbyists help by bringing knowledge to the chaos.

A state lobbyist who has other non-university clients (most institutions do not hire state lobbyists who also represent sister state institutions, although that distinction does not really matter at the federal level) will cost an institution at least $30,000 per year. The lobbyist could cost significantly more, but seldom does she cost less. The investment is worthwhile if the institution's government relations officer charged with taking care of state legislation is not physically based in the capital. Larger institutions must have someone "on the ground," as the saying goes, every day at the statehouse.

Supporting the Alma Mater

States support their community colleges and state universities as well as their private universities. Their doing so is a historic obligation to the state's general welfare. Citizens who become politicians, business owners, teachers, engineers, lawyers, and physicians are often graduates of the state's higher education institutions. They follow the athletic teams and support the alumni associations.

Because of the strong role they play in society, universities expect to be treated well by their state's governor and state legislators. Indeed, in face-to-face meetings with politicians, university presidents are always treated with reverence. (I have witnessed governors hugging university presidents—it is not a pretty sight.) Sometimes, this show of reverence tends to lull universities into complacency and inaction at the state level. Universities are often unprepared when there is a sudden budget cut, or when a legislator introduces legislation that negatively affects higher education.

Employing state lobbyists will provide a front-line defense against surprises that negatively impact the university. Lobbyists cannot guarantee that bad things will not happen, or at least will not be proposed. And lobbyists should not be used as a substitute for a staffed government relations office on campus. Yet with the amount of money at stake (and since many states already have centralized state higher education offices such as boards of regents), it is vital that individual campuses know what is happening, at all times, at the state level.

Local Lobbyists: A Necessary Luxury?

The job of lobbyists working on city and county issues is quite different from what state and federal lobbyists do. A local lobbyist is not going to look for earmarks, or protect state subsidy. Instead, she will work to make the university a cooperative partner with city and county government. An effective local lobbyist can go where no university official (including government relations officers) can—or even should—go. For example, a senior university official should not attend a neighborhood political meeting, or a fund-raising event for a city council candidate, because the university should be viewed as officially politically neutral. But these are exactly the types of events where valuable information is exchanged, from wild gossip to a looming problem on the next zoning board agenda, so having local lobbyists attend such events can be of great benefit to the university.

A local lobbyist can also identify for the university administration who the up-and-coming area politicians are, and how they should be courted by the institution. Many state legislators can trace their political roots back to being first elected to the city council or serving as a county commissioner. Getting future state legislators on campus is a real plus, since it helps shape their views of higher education. And even if the local politician is an alum or has lived near the university all her life, she may not understand the many state issues affecting the university.

Local lobbyists are increasingly involved in the university's role in stimulating economic development. In fact, an especially effective local lobbyist may get himself appointed to one or more economic development boards, to help manage the university's participation in local economic development, thus to gain the best results for the institution.

Who are the local lobbyists? Local lobbyists usually work part-time, and in comparison to their federal counterparts are not very expensive ($2,000 to $3,000 per month without benefits). Able to work under the radar screen, the best local lobbyists often come from the public sector and are generally very young, or are retirees.

The university president and the university government relations officers should inform city and county political leaders that the person will be working for the university. As is typical in politics, somebody will be unhappy with your choice. It is virtually impossible to find a local politician who has not ruffled someone's feathers along the way.

An alternative to a local lobbyist, especially if your university is in a smaller community, is to tap a recently retired university administrator or faculty member. This person brings knowledge of both the university and the town to the table, and might not be burdened with excessive political baggage. Just make certain that the person is not planning to spend all winter (when political action is usually the heaviest) in some warmer climate.

University Lobbying Q & A
Should the University Form a Political Action Committee?

Political action committees (PACs) are not usually viable options for institutions of higher education. PACs are problematic for government relations officers, because board members and alumni sometimes encourage the university president to create a PAC in order to contribute to candidates and other politicians. Whether it is legal or illegal, institutions of higher education do not generally form PACs. Even if a university could or did, who would contribute? Administrators? Faculty members? Students? It is just not feasible. Government relations officers may have to contend with PACs that have been formed to support their university or education issues. For example, what is one supposed to do when an alumni group establishes a PAC to support the university? The university cannot stop them from doing so, or tell them what to do. What if this PAC lobbies for a new basketball arena, which is not a university priority? These are sticky problems that only a president can solve, and even he or she may not be able to make it go away.

Can I Contribute to a Candidate?

Politicians regularly solicit donations from government relations officers. Apart from the obvious prohibition of using a university check or university foundation check, there is nothing wrong with writing a personal check, just so long as you understand that this is a personal contribution, and that you cannot be reimbursed for it. But a government relations officer must be selective and support candidates who support the university or who are at least supporters of important education initiatives. Politicians do not expect you to go to all their fund-raisers. But you will find that you do not have to pay the advertised price if you do go. A donation of fifty dollars instead of two hundred and fifty is acceptable, especially if the event is just a drop-in.

What If a Politician Insists on a Favor?

Like flavors of ice cream, political favors come in many varieties. If the politician has an elderly mother and wants a specialist at your medical center to see her, arrange it. But if the politician then asks to have the hospital and physician charges disappear, respectfully decline. If the politician's nephew has applied to your university, it is appropriate to let the admissions staff know. But then do not interfere with the process (do not give the politician progress reports or tell the politician whether or not his nephew has been admitted). In other matters, such as free tickets to athletic events, understand the ethics laws and follow them to the letter (and be prepared to quote them to the politician if necessary). Perhaps I have been lucky, or have been surrounded by exceptionally honest politicians, but I have had surprisingly few instances of politicians asking for inappropriate favors. This may be the case nationally, given the increasingly stringent lobbying/ethics laws enacted in states and by the federal government.

Should I Worry about Ethics Laws?

You bet. The government relations officer is responsible for making certain not only that she is following state and federal ethics and lobbying laws, but that the rest of the university (including athletics) is following them, as well. The government relations officer's ally is the university attorney or general counsel, who should be able to cite chapter and verse concerning state and federal lobbying rules. It is also the government relations officer's duty to file all necessary ethics reports in a timely fashion. Usually, state ethics commissions require that reports be filed at some regular intervals by lobbyists (including you!) and that they detail any activities with politicians that include a financial expenditure.

What about Earmarks?

I used to think that the term "earmark" came from turning down the corner of a page of a book to keep your place. In other words, a legislator was simply earmarking a page where there was a specifically directed allocation. Apparently, however, earmarking is an animal husbandry practice whereby you attach a metal clip to an ear of a domestic animal like a hog or a cow. Ouch! I hope no one adopts that practice for keeping track of government relations officers.

Really, Isn't It Unseemly for Higher Education to Lobby?

Maybe. Allow me to quote briefly from the public resources page of the American League of Lobbyists' Web site (www.alldc.org/publicresources/lobbying.cfm). The heading at the top of the page reads: "What Is Lobbying?" In the text is the following statement: "Because the lobbying profession is so little understood, it is often viewed as a sinister function, yet every 'mom and apple pie' interest in the United States uses lobbyists—a fact little known by the general public."

The truth of the matter is that government at all levels is too complicated and there is too much money on the table—$18.3 billion was spent on federal earmarks in fiscal year 2008—not to use honest professional lobbyists to gain higher education's fair share (see www.businessandme dia.org/printer/2008/20080220134418.aspx).

CHAPTER SEVEN

Free Lunches

The Higher Education Associations

Peter McPherson, president of the National Association of State Universities and Land-Grant Colleges (NASULGC), had a problem. At NASULGC's quarterly meeting, about sixty government relations officers, mostly from larger research universities, were doing what they do best: drinking coffee, gossiping, and checking e-mail while paying partial attention to informal panels about current legislative topics. Everybody sat up straighter, though, when Dr. McPherson unexpectedly entered the room.

The soft-spoken and sophisticated president of the association said that he needed some advice, which could presumably be about any one of a number of important higher education issues being discussed in Washington. Most pressing at the time was the debate over the mammoth and complex Higher Education Reauthorization Act, whose fate had just become more complicated with the announcement of Senator Edward Kennedy's brain tumor and prognosis. Opinion was divided among the government relations officers whether Kennedy's illness would mean the bill would have smoother sailing because of sympathy for Kennedy, or would flounder because he would not be present to guide it to passage. Maybe the NASULGC president would have an opinion.

Dr. McPherson, however, had a different problem to discuss: the staff and board of NASULGC had been wrestling for some time with a proposed change in the association's name, not to mention its tortured acronym. The name originally evolved in 1963 when the American Association of Land-Grant Colleges and Universities merged with the National Association of State Universities. But the awkward name has always been a burden for the organization, which is one of the members of what is commonly known as the "Big Six" associations of higher education in Washington. The name is not as elegant as, say, the American Council on Education (ACE). Further, the term "Land-Grant" carries less weight and meaning in today's education circles than in decades past. Dr. McPherson suggested some alternative names, but none seemed to hit the right note. After a few more minutes of pleasant chatting, he thanked the group and left.

What is going on here!? One might wonder if the emperor is fiddling while Rome is burning. But Dr. McPherson, who has worked in senior executive positions with the U.S. government and Bank of America, and was president of Michigan State University, is no fool. His visit to the government relations officers' meeting is symbolic of the complex world that exists among the associations, agencies, lobbyists, and individuals in Washington whose raison d'être is higher education.

An organization's name change is an insider's decision. Top executives and the board make the decision, although there might be some input from a consultant or some external organization like a marketing firm. There are crucial aspects of a name change that must be considered: (1) historical context; (2) possible confusion resulting from a name change; (3) the expense of changing everything from building signage to stationery to lapel pins; and (4) whether employees and institutional members across the country would resent the change.

By floating the name change to a group of government relations officers, Dr. McPherson knew he would be getting the subject in front of all of the presidents of the universities represented. It would actually be a more effective ploy than simply writing to all the presidents represented (which he very well might have done, although I never saw such a letter at my university). Government relations officers—especially those who live in or travel to Washington—love secrets. And a proposed name change has that aura of a secret. Further, the holder of the secret demonstrates that he or she has an inside track. I would wager that every government relations officer informed his or her president about the change presumably imminent at NASULGC.

But still, such secrecy begs the question of why a name change would be important. The answer to that question goes to an understanding of the relationships and differences among the Big Six major higher education associations, as well as how these associations relate to the other, more focused, often discipline-oriented associations located in Washington. Sometimes the Big Six associations are collectively referred to as One Dupont Circle, the home address of the ACE and a few other higher education associations. The other members of the Big Six besides NASULGC and ACE are the Association of American Universities (AAU), the National Association of Independent Colleges and Universities (NAICU), the American Association of State Colleges and Universities (AASCU), and the American Association of Community Colleges (AACC).

The higher education associations in Washington have been around long enough—some since the turn of the twentieth century—that they have cooperatively carved out their own specific niches in higher education. Obviously, one major player deals with two-year schools, including community and junior colleges. Another player deals only with private universities. Although the others mostly represent public universities, they specialize to some extent in research or in general education. Higher education associations also all have their own professional programs, such as the ACE fellowship program, which provides leadership training for future administrators, university presidents, and provosts. Most of the associations publish pamphlets or monographs from time to time. All of them hold very nice meetings in desirable locations.

The associations pride themselves on showing a united front to Congress and the administration. For example, less than five weeks before the 2008 presidential election, an article from the September 25 edition of *Inside Higher Ed* reported:

> The presidents of six national higher education groups have sent a joint letter to the presidential candidates outlining ideas for ways that colleges could work with the next administration. The ideas generally repeat statements that the association leaders have made previously, calling for a renewed emphasis on access to college, greater "transparency" to help prospective students and families make decisions about colleges, support for research and job training to promote economic competitiveness, and backing of international education as a diplomatic tool.

These are not profound thoughts. I am certain the dairy lobbyists sent the candidates their own "ideas for ways that the [dairy industry] could work

From Sore Throat to a Sneeze

The National Association of State Universities and Land-Grant Colleges changed its name at the association's national meeting on November 10, 2008. The new name, the Association of Public and Land-Grant Universities, is to be said by pronouncing the letters *A-P-L-U* separately, instead of trying to say the letters as a word, which comes out like a sneeze, according to one blogger (*Chronicle of Higher Education,* November 28, 2008). In a press release, APLU President Peter McPherson explained that the "goal was to rebrand the organization while maintaining our core values and identity." The press release details the extraordinary lengths that the association went to in order to have the name thoroughly vetted: "The process to change the name began one year ago with the convening of an ad-hoc committee of former board chairs. NASULGC staff conducted an initial survey of members and select external target audience members in the spring. The Board of Directors and the Council of Presidents held further discussion in June. More extensive market research was conducted in August and September by the higher education marketing firm SimpsonScarborough. In October, comment was solicited from the entire membership." About the only vetting the press release leaves out was Dr. McPherson's asking the advice of us government relations officers. Well, thank you very much. Gesundheit!

with the next administration." Still, the education associations were presenting a united front to the candidates and alerting the winner to the strength and complexity of American higher education.

Nevertheless, competition does exist among the associations, and something like an association name change would signal disruption of the status quo. (Much like *Star Wars'* Obi-Wan Kenobi sensing a disturbance in the Force.) Does a name change indicate a new direction or mission for NASULGC? Could it mean a takeover or merging of NASULGC with another association? Might it suggest that NASULGC will pursue a new relationship with its member universities, or maybe make a marketing push to steal some university memberships? Does a name change signal a major expansion of its staff, or possibly even a staff shakeup?

This is serious stuff. After all, in 2007 the American Association for Higher Education got a psychological jump on everyone else by adding "and Accreditation" to its name.

Was Dr. McPherson testing the waters in front of the government relations officers? Those from outside the beltway would probably know little about the implications of the name change, but a third of the government relations officers in attendance were based in Washington. As insiders, they might have a better sense of some of the questions above. As insiders, they might pick up on the president's signals that it would be all right to come over during the cocktail hour and whisper in his ear.

The Big Six and the larger discipline-only associations—such as the Association of American Medical Colleges, the National Association of College and University Business Officers, and the National Council of University Research Administrators—are at the apex of government relations and higher education. This is the Major League, where the defenders of the greatest education system in the world guard against the powers of the greatest democracy in the world. (You might have thought that they would be on the same page, but often they are not.) Whether presidents, government relations officers, and lobbyists work for the Ohio State University or Ohio Wesleyan, for Ohio University or Ohio Northern University, their efforts pale before the titanic struggles between the higher education associations in Washington and the federal government.

And this is where the notion of free lunches surfaces.

An article by Ben Adler in the September 2007 issue of *Washington Monthly* (Washingtonmonthly.com/features/2007/0709.adler) caused quite a stir in the Washington education establishment. Entitled "Inside the Higher Ed Lobby: Welcome to One Dupont Circle, Where Good Education-Reform Ideas Go to Die," the article outlines how education associations speak with one voice, one that essentially advocates for a status quo that opposes most legislation reforms, from admission standards to tuition rates. Adler asserts that the associations are so entrenched in Washington that they don't even have to spend much money on lobbying. Instead, the education establishment

wields power in two effective if subtle ways. First it plays an inside game, conducting quiet, sit-down meetings with policy makers in which it trades on its expertise on the often technical questions of education policy. . . . Second, higher ed makes skillful use of its hometown ties [since] legislators often have a soft spot for their alma mater, or for the state university whose football team they grew up rooting for.

In other words, the associations tackle the broad education issues that affect the greatest number of member universities. They deal with large dollar amounts, such as what the final figure will be for the Federal Pell Grants. They halt maverick amendments that might cap tuition. They keep a lame-duck secretary of education from having too much influence over policy. These are issues and battles that those of us at Ordinary State University and Really Small Private College are only dimly aware are even taking place.

A few of us government relations officers do make it occasionally to Washington, and we do avail ourselves of the hospitalities of one or another of the national associations that our university or college belongs to. We even offer opinions to association staff who deign to meet with us. (It is in their job descriptions to do so.) But we are fooling ourselves and our presidents back home if we imply that we are having much, if any, influence on Washington policy. So, this is the challenge faced in the government relations and presidents' offices of all the 4,000 universities that exist in the United States outside of Washington. Should your institution have a presence in Washington where you can have your voice heard on issues beyond those that specifically affect and benefit your own institution?

A number of factors that partially define the scope and makeup of your institution's office of government relations can help answer this question:

- *The ambition level of your institution's president and provost.* If your president and/or provost are interested in eventually moving from your university to another, larger or more prestigious university, then Washington networking and connections can be essential. (The university's government relations officer is often the *only* person to know that the university president is job-hunting.) Although many major education head-hunting firms are based in the city, being on association boards, committees, and study groups is an important professional credential for a president. Of all senior administrators, a government relations officer should recognize this ambition and provide plenty of opportunities for the president/pro-vost to travel to Washington and participate in association work.

- *The role of your congressperson.* If your university is in the district of a congressperson who is a party leader, or if she sits on an education/research committee, is a Cardinal, or otherwise serves on Appropriations, you, the government relations officer, owe it to the associations and all of higher education to be active in Washington. In this case, your congressperson is obligated to pay attention to you—probably a lot more of attention than she would pay to a university representative from the other side of the country, or to representatives from the Big Six. Even if the congressperson has not particularly done much for your university, you still have greater access to the congressperson and her staff than most people in Washington. It may be up to you to carry higher education's message to the congressperson.

- *A crucial back-home issue.* Though most federal issues are broad policy issues, every once in a while there comes along something that specifically will affect a small group of schools, or maybe even only your school. (This goes back to the point I made in chapter 6, where success might be defined as changing just one sentence of an 1,158-page bill, which is the length of the Higher Education Reauthorization Act.) An association may be able to provide insight and valuable contacts in making that change happen.

- *Your university's reputation.* If your university has no presence in Washington, and only a limited government relations budget, membership in an association may be the cheapest way to get your university's name out there. Does a small Midwestern state university need to be known in Washington to continue its day-to-day existence? Of course not. If the institution decides for whatever reason to take the next step up, however, having a presence in Washington should be part of the strategy.

If it is still not practical or necessary for any of the above reasons for your university to make a splash in Washington, there are nonetheless benefits from belonging to one of the Big Six or other national higher education associations. One is a constant barrage of e-mail alerts. Albeit occasionally annoying, e-mail alerts provide the government relations officer with information about higher education congressional legislation and other Washington happenings. Association conferences and workshops can provide indispensable networking opportunities, not to mention pleasant vacation destinations.

I would be remiss if I did not point out another extremely important role performed by the Big Six higher education associations in Washington. From time to time, they all issue short reports—variously called white papers, study documents, policy briefs, or something similar—that provide comprehensive analysis of current issues in higher education. For example, at this moment on my desk I have a discussion paper from NASULGC entitled "University Tuition, Consumer Choice and College Affordability: Strategies for Addressing a Higher Education Affordability Challenge." I also have an 88-page booklet from the Association of Academic Health Centers entitled "Out of Order, Out of Time: The State of the Nation's Health Workforce." Another working paper from the American Council on Education covers international partnerships among colleges and universities. Such reports are not only valuable for appropriate campus personnel, but they are excellent resources for senators, congresspersons, and their staff members.

Although some of the large higher education associations in Washington struggle to get along, aligning themselves against flawed federal education legislation while informing their university constituents across the nation, there is no such similar effort at the state and local levels (although the National Association of Independent Colleges and Universities has the equivalent of branch associations in states). There are, of course, administrative offices and discipline-specific associations that operate nationally, regionally, and in states, such as the National Association of College and University Business Officers and the National Association of College and University Attorneys. Still, government relations officers should make a point of staying in touch with campus representatives to these groups, especially when a local issue has the potential of becoming a national issue.

It is important that the public university government relations officer understand the political reasons for the lack of state-level higher education associations. Within most states, three political decisions have helped

Look Them Up on the Web (If You Don't Believe Me)

A number of higher education associations in Washington are not members of the Big Six. Highlighted below are just a few of the dozens, if not hundreds, of national higher education groups lobbying in our nation's capital. You may be curious if they are lobbying for or against policies favored by your university. Check them out.

The Council for Opportunity in Education (www.coenet.us) works with institutions that "host TRIO Programs to specifically help low-income students enter college and graduate." TRIO programs such as Upward Bound "help students to overcome class, social, academic, and cultural barriers to higher education." The COE government relations staff hosts conference calls about Washington happenings weekly.

EDUCAUSE (www.educause.edu) has a mission to "advance higher education by promoting the intelligent use of information technology." One member from an elite Midwestern private university gave this testimonial: "When I go out on a technological limb, I know I have a diverse community of practice to turn to for timely information and advice through EDUCAUSE constituency groups, publications and online resources."

The Council on Governmental Relations (www.cogr.edu), founded in 1948, is involved in all aspects of federal research for its 150 member institutions. COGR claims that its "primary function is to provide advice and information to its membership and to make certain that federal agencies understand academic operations and the impact of proposed regulations on colleges and universities."

NAFSA: Association of International Educators (www.nafsa.org) promotes the volunteer nature of its organization by asserting that "hundreds of NAFSA members volunteer each year to serve the association to create and disseminate knowledge, to influence international education policy, and to maintain a strong organization." Its sixtieth conference in May 2008 attracted 9,400 participants from 110 countries to Washington. NAFSA stands for the original name of the National Association of Foreign Student Advisers.

The Council of Graduate Schools (www.cgsnet.org) is part of the One Dupont Circle crowd. Five hundred universities in the United States and Canada belong to CGS, which has "the mission to advance graduate edu-

cation in order to ensure the vitality of intellectual discovery and to promote an environment that cultivates rigorous scholarship." The 2008
CGS summer workshop, which was held in Vail, Colorado, attracted 250
deans.

---

to prevent (or at least limit) the practicality of forming effective state associations that had any clout with state government, or for that matter any
clout with other statewide entities such as labor unions: (1) universities
consciously choosing not to involve themselves in state political actions,
preferring to trust in the state's largess as it pertains to funding; (2) universities deferring to the largest university, which is often located in the
state capital, with the idea that it would be useless to try to compete, and
that the "flagship" university would never harm its smaller sister schools;
and (3) the creation by legislation of a board of regents or board of governors that would oversee higher education in the state.

The first two reasons discussed above have largely diminished over
the past decade. Few universities believe they can prosper by avoiding
being politically active. Similarly, in today's legislative environment, no
one trusts that the flagship universities will help their smaller sister institutions. (The Cinderella metaphor is more applicable here than *Little
Women*.) However, the rise of the oversight boards has been a crucial development that will have increasing impact on both public *and private*
higher education in the future.

It is impossible to categorize the subtle nuances between public oversight state boards (which are often called regents). It is also unnecessary
to do. Few, if any, university presidents or government relations officers
work in more than one state at a time. About the only time that sharing
information between state systems might be necessary is if the governor
and/or legislature contemplate changing the governing board's structure.
Such an event happened in Ohio in 2007, when a new governor took office and charted a plan to reorganize the 40-year-old Ohio Board of Regents. Following the governor's announcement, senior public university
administrators in Ohio desperately tried to determine which state was
being used as a model for the new regents and the new University System of Ohio. The governor and his newly appointed chancellor in due

course created a hybrid that most senior administrators felt was a combination of the system in Maryland with that in Florida.

Whatever shape it takes, a state's board of regents will declare in its mission statement and strategic plan that it exists to support higher education. In this regard, these boards function similarly in their relationship to state governments as do the large higher education associations in Washington function in their relationships to the federal government. The boards are advocates for higher education to the governor/legislators. They sometimes assume the role of mediators between higher education and the governor/legislators. And they take on tough state issues that most universities would not be able or equipped to handle alone.

In terms of government function, the contact person between a university and a typical board of regents should be the university's government relations officer responsible for covering state politics. But this is not always the case (the relationship between the regents and individual universities is confusing and complex where it should be clear), because regents almost always have responsibilities lying beyond just being a cheerleader (or guardian) for higher education in the state.

Boards of regents typically have three components. There are the regents themselves, in most cases appointed by the governor, but in some cases elected. Sometimes, one or two legislators have seats on the boards. Regents may have specified duties (granted either by the governor or by law), or they may be only advisory. Next, there is an administrative head, sometimes called a chancellor, who also has varying degrees of power by state statute from state to state. Finally, there is the staff, which takes care of everything from office work to setting higher education policy to managing higher education finances.

The jobs of making policy and managing finances are where boards of regents are fundamentally different from the Washington associations. And this is also where all sorts of university administrators beyond government relations officers become involved with the regents. Take degree approval, for example. Legislators in many states became aware over the years that state universities offered duplicative degrees. For some reason, doctoral programs in history were often the degrees targeted. (Just how many Ph.D.s in history did a state need, anyhow?) Some state legislatures gave regents the power to approve all degree programs from state universities (and sometimes from private universities in the state, as well) and thereby to ensure less duplication and better use of academic resources. Of course, a lot of people on campuses did not appreciate this type of academic management from the legislature—especially history faculty members, chairs of history departments, undergraduate and graduate history students, provosts, and presidents. They directly petitioned chancellors, regents, and regent staffers on these issues while seldom appealing to government relations officers for assistance. For the most part, administrators, faculty, and students were unsuccessful in gaining reconsideration except for an occasional postponement to do another study. Again, decisions were made without involving government relations offices.

Should government relations officers become enmeshed in regents' issues? The doctoral program in history mentioned above is a curricular issue that should be the purview of provosts and faculties. Yet it was initiated by legislative action. But what action? What if the Speaker of the House and/or the President of the Senate, instead of writing legislation, were to meet with the chancellor and "suggest" that the history "problem" be solved? Where does a university government relations officer insert himself into this process? Frankly, it would be difficult. But if a House member introduces legislation about history, then a watchful government relations officer might do any number of things, like convincing the legislator (for sound reasons) to withdraw the bill, or having the legislator's party kill it in caucus before the bill moves forward.

In other words, deciding *who* manages the relationship between the university and the board of regents is very complicated. Yet far too many universities allow this management concern to drift along, with too few people paying too little attention, until suddenly a history doctoral program disappears, or a funding subsidy formula is changed, or regent-controlled research funds go to a sister school. Sometimes, senior administrators defer to their president to speak directly to the chancellor, whether for information or for problem solving. But because of busy schedules, these conversations do not always happen, and there is often a need for a better communications system. Management concerns of this sort do not necessarily have to be undertaken by the government relations officer (and may be too complex or too technical for him to undertake anyway), but that person—whoever it proves to be—should be part of a senior leadership team that maintains a good relationship with the regents.

In some states, public universities have formed their own associations for state lobbying activities. Chapter 1 describes Ohio's Inter-University Council, whose existence predated the legislative creation of the Ohio Board of Regents by nearly 30 years. Such organizations are fairly rare and seldom address all aspects of higher education in a state. What happens more often is that individual university administrators—particularly in fields of research—form groups to lobby for directed funding or collaborative projects. Interestingly enough, these groups cut across the public and private university sectors in order to gain certain expertise and broader support.

Every university government relations officer has received a variation of the following phone call:

> Hi, my name is Mary Smith. I'm a faculty member in the College of Education and this year I'm the president of the state Association of the American United Federation of College of Education Tenure Faculty Members Interested in the Promotion of Effective Teaching, or AAUFCETFMIPET for short. I have two requests: First, we'd like the governor to speak next week at our state conference. Also, since I am AAUFCETFMIPET's president, I must request that all our state legislators vote to increase funding for Colleges of Education in next year's budget. Can you help us?

Okay, I admit that I made up some of that. But believe me, I did not make up the requests. There is no question that associations—whether national or local, whether broad-based or narrowly-focused—play an important role in today's higher education landscape. In fact, they have played that role for some time. But with the rise of offices of government relations, increased coordination and participation, sorely needed, can be achieved. After all, everyone is working toward the same goals. (I think.)

CHAPTER EIGHT

Community Colleges, Private Universities, and Signs of the Apocalypse

Every week, *Sports Illustrated* reports a sports-related happening so bizarre that it must signal in some way that the end of the world is near. From the March 30, 2009, issue: "Police in Indiana drove a high school basketball coach 45 miles to his team's playoff game after he posted bond on a DWI charge." Community colleges and private universities, which are seldom mentioned in the same academic breath, are also facing signs of the apocalypse. These institutions are important and essential segments in the vast tapestry of higher education in America. In many ways, of course, their concerns are quite different. But they also share some distinct similarities, and this chapter will examine those similarities that community colleges and private universities, at least in terms of the politics of higher education, will be drawn ever closer together in the future.

For a wide variety of students, of all ages, community colleges offer less costly post-secondary education alternatives. They not only provide basic college education to students who then transfer to four-year institutions, but also offer numerous associate degrees (or equivalent workforce training programs) in everything from fire fighting to accounting. The vertical (university transfer)/horizontal (terminal degree) theory of community college education is discussed in detail in *Community Colleges: Policy in the Future Context*, edited by Barbara K. Townsend and Susan B. Twombly.

Private universities generally emphasize the liberal arts. They seek students who generally want a broad liberal arts education, and often provide heritage education for sons and daughters of alumni. Many private university graduates are expected to continue their education at professional schools such as law, medicine, and engineering. Private universities were the first institutions of higher education in America. They often have historic religious components that set them apart from today's secular public higher education.

In other areas—particularly those related to aspects of government relations—the concerns of private universities and community colleges are surprisingly similar. Here are the most notable examples.

Physical Isolation. Many community colleges and private universities are located in rural environments, away from large cities and state capitals. Though these bucolic settings may be ideal for study and learning, they promote an out-of-sight, out-of-mind attitude that reduces political input and influence and awareness.

Small Administrative Staff. Both community colleges and private universities tend to have small senior administrative staff. This is so partly because of the institutions' emphasis on teaching, but also because both community colleges and private universities devote a great deal of their administrative effort to the recruitment of students. Very few smaller community colleges and smaller private universities have an administrator totally dedicated to government relations work, and even larger institutions seldom have a true government relations staff.

Disinterested Faculty. Few faculty members in any segment of higher education are interested in government relations, as discussed in chapter 2, but faculty members at community colleges and private universities tend to be even less interested. This, of course, is no reflection on their excellent teaching abilities. It is just a fact of academic life at community colleges, where faculty members often are part time and have other jobs that they consider their primary employment, and at private universities, where faculty members are engaged not only in research and writing but also in close mentoring relationships with students.

Apolitical Governing Boards. Governing boards at both community colleges and private universities tend to be focused on their institutions' missions, and tend to discourage their administrations from being excessively active in politics. This mindset is somewhat truer of private universities, where board members might come from out of state and not be interested in local/state politics. Community college board members, for their part, may be appointed by the governor or elected by the public, as is true of board members at public four-year state universities. Board members at community colleges that receive local levy funding may by necessity be extremely active in local politics.

Competitive Mindset. In this day and age, all institutions of higher education compete for students, but community colleges go further, jealously protecting what they deem is their territory. Indeed, some states have established community college districts or the equivalent, using a kind of supra-high school district concept. This scheme is supposed to reduce competition among community colleges, but often the competition increases, as each feels the need to protect the territory of its district. The problem for community colleges is that students are not generally restricted, as they may be in high school, to attend only the high school in their district. Private universities, especially small institutions, do not have to worry about being restricted by districts. But they know that they must compete fiercely with other private universities for the relatively small number of top students who desire a private university education. Although competition is a time-honored business practice, it is not favored by many politicians, who prefer that institutions of higher education cooperate and collaborate.

Common Heritage. A small number of community colleges and private universities (as well as some schools that eventually evolved into state-supported institutions) were originally created through the Young Men's Christian Association, or through similar adult learning programs in the early days of the twentieth century. Sometimes known as YMCA colleges or vocational tech schools, these schools tended to be in the larger cities. Over the years, some developed as two-year community colleges (e.g. Sinclair Community College in Dayton), some developed into private universities (e.g. Bradley University in Peoria), and some developed into public institutions (e.g. Cleveland State University).

Closed Presidencies. Presidents (and other senior administrators) of both community colleges and private universities are just as affable and intelligent as those of four-year state universities, but both community colleges and private universities tend to promote from within or hire staff from similar institutions. Four-year universities tend to seek administrators from a wide range of institutions, people who more often than not have at least some expertise and knowledge of practical politics and higher education government relations.

Community colleges and private universities also share another trait: making certain that students have sufficient financial aid to pay for tuition. This is a major political concern for all of these institutions—even the elite private research universities that are necessarily interested in the politics of federal government research funding. Community colleges and smaller, nonresearch private universities depend *primarily* on students being able to pay tuition. I have had private university presidents tell me that tuition is their *only* revenue source. These institutions do not have access to public state subsidy, or to large endowments or the indirect campus costs arising from numerous research grants. They must receive tuition payments from their students if they are to survive year after year.

According to the American Association of Community Colleges, nearly half (47 percent) of community college students receive some sort of financial aid, with much of that aid coming from federal grants and loans, and a smaller portion from state scholarship programs (www2.aacc.nche .edu/research/index.htm). Financial aid is crucial to community college students, even though the annual tuition at these schools is about a third of the cost of tuition at a state university ($2,361 vs. $6,185). Community colleges are dependent on the federal government (and, to a lesser extent, state government) to provide their students with grants and loans. Therefore, securing tuition aid is the main focus of government relations' activities in community colleges.

Meanwhile, the average tuition at four-year private universities is $23,712. Although these schools provide their students with more heritage, academic, and religious scholarships, their students nonetheless depend to a greater or lesser extent on federal grants and loan programs. In fact, according to the 2008 *Chronicle Almanac*, 65 percent of students attending four-year, nondoctorate-granting private universities receive some kind of federal grant and/or loan. In addition, private universities often receive substantial state funding (the equivalent of subsidies, but seldom called subsidies) for in-state residents who attend the universities. This funding generally is not publicized, and is not well known to the citizens of the state. (The idea of privileged students receiving noncompetitive state grants to go to a private university is not a politically attractive notion.) So grant funding is disguised by some euphemistic phrase such as Florida Bright Futures, Kentucky Educational Excellence Scholarships, and Minnesota State Grants. Despite what a scholarship might be named, it still constitutes public funding going to private institutions. John V. Lombardi, the current president of the Louisiana State University System, wrote in the March 3, 2006, edition of *Inside Higher Ed* under the headline "Public and Private: What's the Difference?": "America's private institutions are a public trust. While they can evade many of the considerable bureaucratic and regulatory costs of obligations that public universities endure, they are, nonetheless, publicly subsidized institutions with private governance."

The good news for community college and private university presidents is that campaigning for maintaining or increasing federal loans to their students is generally well received by federal and state officials and politicians. The bad news for community college and private university presidents is that they do not typically have a government relations staff to do the campaigning for them. In most cases, their presidents have to do the work themselves. They have to travel to their state capitals and to Washington. They have to keep current with bills in Congress and the state legislature. They have to monitor the information posted from their national and state associations. And, when necessary, they have to write and send out the letters and e-mails pleading that scholarship and loan funding not be cut.

Often, these are men and women who—as pointed out above—are neither trained nor particularly interested in the political arena. In addition, their constituencies of board members, faculty, and even students are not necessarily supportive of such activities, much less helpful with them. One president of a private university whom I interviewed told me somewhat apologetically that because his school is too small to have a provost, he was performing those duties, as well. With an enrollment under one thousand, this president relies on the director of the state branch of the National Association of Independent Colleges and Universities to lobby for the school. Fortunately, the president said, in his opinion the director does an excellent job.

What is so apocalyptic about this current state of affairs? Why is the

end of the world imminent for community colleges and private universities? All right, I'm being a bit melodramatic. But important changes in
higher education are squeezing community colleges and private universities from both ends of the academic and economic continuum. Many of
these changes have a political component that cannot be ignored.

An ongoing example of community college squeeze is the debate
about the future of two-year institutions. This debate, which varies from
state to state, is complicated by the fact that a broad range of institutions
(and even whole education systems) have evolved for students who are
between graduating from high school and attending a four-year college.
There are community colleges, junior colleges, two-year university branch
campuses, technical colleges, on-line colleges, and variously named adult
learning centers. (Sometimes, two or more of these schools actually share
buildings and campuses.) All of this, of course, makes mission differen-
tiation murky at best.

So, what is the mission of the two-year institution? Allow me to over-
simplify. Community college traditionalists would assert that the institution's mission is to train a skilled workforce. Nursing assistants. Trades
people. Safety and emergency personnel. Technical specialties. Training
a skilled workforce is a valid and important societal function. One community college president told me that welders were so sorely needed in
his region that many students who enrolled in his college's two-year master welding program were offered high-paying jobs after completing *just
one class,* and accordingly opted not to stay in school. The president was
concerned that such employment might be good for students in the short
run, but not so great for them over time. The exodus also played havoc
with his college's efforts to plan its welding program's curriculum, enrollment, and staffing.

Many community college presidents have come to believe that community colleges should evolve into a whole new system of four-year colleges. Led by Florida's community colleges, this movement to extend the
scope of the community college system is now advocated all over America, particularly by urban community colleges that have large physical
campuses (and, sometimes, athletic teams). With the added incentive of
funding through local levies and/or sale taxes, this shift is almost a rein-
vention of the city universities of the mid-twentieth century.

Signs of the Higher Education Apocalypse

- According to a report from the Ohio Board of Regents, the 2006 fall enrollment in Ohio community colleges was 172,118, but during that academic year, ending in July 2007, only 13,717 degrees were awarded.
- Testifying before Congress on May 1, 2008, Dr. Wayne Watson, Chancellor of City Colleges of Chicago, stated "Many policymakers are still surprised to learn that community colleges enroll 47 percent of all U.S undergraduates."
- The University of Phoenix is the country's largest private university, and although it does not have any athletic teams, it has paid to put its name on the new arena in Glendale, Arizona, where the 2007 BCS national football championship was played.
- An Iowa community college president was fired but given a $400,000 severance package after trustees viewed a published photo of him pouring beer into a young woman's mouth. (current.com/items/89247797).

The third mission being handed the community colleges is much more political (and, do I dare say, apocalyptic?). Officials in state government—in particular, the executive and legislative branches—generally view community colleges as two-year feeder schools for average students hoping to transition into a traditional university education. Higher-achieving students, for their part, go straight to the four-year universities in pursuit of degrees that will prepare them for the twenty-first-century workforce. In other words, community colleges are becoming (for both students and the state) inexpensive vertical conduits to state universities, which will themselves become high-tech job-oriented training centers.

Government relations officers (or presidents acting in this role) at community colleges are faced with a number of political dilemmas. First, they have less clout than their four-year university brethren. In the minds of many state legislators, the smallest four-year state university takes priority over the largest two-year state community college. Second, the government relations officer/president must have a firm understanding of his or her institution's mission, both as gleaned from the guidance of trustees and as it relates to peer institutions. Third, they must be able to develop a viable political agenda on the basis of that mission. Whatever that mission might be for community colleges, politically it must include open admission, because politically that is the most important card that two-year institutions hold. Whether the community college trains welders, grants four-year degrees, or passes students on to universities (or tries to do all three), the community college must never say to government that it will turn away the least prepared students who come to its door.

Meanwhile, private universities (even the smallest ones) do turn away students. Lots of them. When asked, private university administrators acknowledge that many of the highly motivated students they turn away just end up at another institution. Legislators and the general public are not usually concerned that private universities are not educating enough students. But it is *what* they are teaching their students that gives rise to their apocalyptic political circumstance.

Many states have one or more public universities that function much like private universities. Sometimes, these universities are called "Public Ivies" in the tradition of the eight Ivy League universities. In Ohio, that school is Miami University, located in Oxford, Ohio, which is better known as Miami of Ohio (note that neither name includes the word "state"). The very first sentence of Miami's mission statement includes the words "unwavering commitment to liberal arts undergraduate education" (www .miami.muohio.edu/president/mission/). Miami president David Hodge said in his annual fall address in 2008 that "the class-based academic experience is the most central activity" to "advancing the Miami Experience" (www.miami.muohio.edu/president/reports_and_speeches/pdfs/Engaged_ University_and_Student_Success.pdf).

At the present time, however, President Hodge and Miami of Ohio are under tremendous pressure from the Ohio Board of Regents and state officials and legislators to alter the university's mission, thus to be more of what might be described as a "team player" in the newly created University System of Ohio. No one questions the academic achievements of Miami's faculty or students. But can—or will—Miami of Ohio help carry out the Ohio Board of Regents' strategic plan to increase enrollment at

Ohio universities dramatically, and to stimulate Ohio's economic development through applied research and workforce training? In other words, how is a commitment to liberal arts going to help an out-of-work Dayton factory employee forty miles away from Oxford, Ohio?

It may seem odd that I am writing about a public university here instead of a private university. But what is happening to Miami of Ohio and other Public Ivies around the country may very well be a bellwether for what will be happening to private universities in the near future. A public university is just an easier target for legislators. Of course, Miami of Ohio receives millions of dollars in state student subsidy, as well as significant state and federal funding for scholarships, research, and building construction. And most private universities also receive significant public funding. At least Miami of Ohio recognizes this public funding and its obligations to the state. Private universities seek to downplay or obfuscate this fact.

The dilemma, then, both for private universities and for Public Ivies, is how to engage the core liberal arts faculty and convince them that societal pressures as represented by government demands need not necessarily destroy traditional university education as envisioned by the faculty. This is a major problem for these schools, because ultimately it strikes at the heart of curriculum, which, even more than in public universities, is the sole domain of the faculty. This new desideratum is more than just offering a couple of "tech writing" courses in the English department. It is an entire restructuring of the core courses taught to freshmen and sophomores, with a realigning of subject matter for juniors and seniors and the addition of a universal internship/co-op requirement. Few liberal arts faculties want to do this, or will allow it to be done to them by administration.

Needless to say, a government relations officer cannot do much about this pending internecine warfare. However, a government relations effort is exactly what is needed to negotiate the waters among government officials, who are increasingly concerned about how tax revenues are spent, and faculty members, who do not agree with President Lombardi's words (four pages back) that private universities are just public universities in disguise. If private university presidents do not know how to do this themselves, and if they cannot afford to hire their own government relations staffs, then their only recourse (besides ignoring the crisis) is to have their association representatives do it for them. One private university president said as much to me, and added that he thought his association lobbyist did a great job. "Our guy always says that his only job is babysitting our money," he remarked.

Well, that's fine, but it's only half the job. Private university leaders must gain the support of their faculty and be more conscious and accepting of government's new interest in accountability and economic development. They need to recognize that their institutions must be bigger players in local governmental affairs. When questioned about this, one private university president told me proudly that he had appointed an administrator with the title vice president for development and public affairs. But when I asked about the vice president's job duties, the president admitted that the administrator spent ninety percent of his time doing development and ten percent doing public affairs.

Some private university presidents have a better understanding of public affairs, or at least are more proactive and willing to take political risks for political benefits. Kendall L. Baker, president of Ohio Northern University, knew that because Ohio Northern is the largest employer in the institution's home county, the university had an obligation to be a good citizen. This meant purchasing fire-fighting and EMS equipment for county use. "Private university focus is changing a good deal," Dr. Baker asserted, "and remodeling our community infrastructure is changing the area's perception of ONU."

The Apocalypse

For many readers, the most certain sign of the apocalypse may be that I have dared to write about community colleges and private universities, as well as occasionally mentioning four-year public universities, all in the same chapter. Although many faculty members and administrators would protest vehemently, there are few institutions in America that are more class conscious and stratified than higher education. Higher education shamelessly uses the backgrounds of students to avoid being labeled as class conscious. Rich kids are able to enroll at a community college. Poor kids are welcomed at a prestigious private university. But in interacting with each other and in their relationships with the many levels of governments, the entities of higher education eschew working together for a common good.

Clark Kerr called this the "segmentation" of higher education, and he believed it would only become worse in the twenty-first century. Segmentation is so ingrained in the people who run higher education that they do not even know they are doing it. Frank T. Rhodes' book *The Creation of the Future* is relevant to anyone working in any institution of higher education. Yet, Dr. Rhodes says in his introduction, "I confine myself to the 125 or so institutions that are often called 'major research universities,' places where professors and their graduate students—the professionals and professors of tomorrow—are actively engaged in original scholarship and research and professional service, as well as teaching the accumulated knowledge of the present and past" (p. xiii). I am sure that Dr. Rhodes and Cornell University Press were hoping that more than "125 or so" copies of the book would be sold, because one can open it at random and find a topic relevant to all of higher education. For example, on page 155, he writes, "It is time to unbundle tenure and compensation." Surely tenure and compensation are issues that extend far beyond the "125 or so" major research universities.

Dr. Rhodes, of course, is not alone in being emotionally stuck in one gear while being able intellectually to understand (and write about) a great deal more. Higher education must break through these artificial strata. It must stop cooperating with *U.S. News* and other magazines and Web sites that profit by establishing artificial ranking criteria and then pitting institutions against one another. Our administrative forefathers in higher education should have been smarter than to get suckered into that process years ago. The institutions of higher education cannot survive politically unless they rid themselves of artificial barriers between and among themselves. President Baker of Ohio Northern University said to me that "In the last ten years, the private university presidents are more politically sensitive and politically savvy." I believe that is true. I believe it is also true of community college presidents and public four-year university presidents. The problem is that, for the most part, *none* of the presidents know what to do. Essentially, they are fighting a rear guard action while squabbling among themselves and with their faculties. Presidents do have some allies. Increasing numbers of legislators are turning to higher education for economic assistance. Trustees are becoming more knowledgeable about their responsibilities. More faculty members can see beyond the limits of their own departments and colleges. And a growing cadre of higher education-oriented government relations officers have come to understand the complexities of both higher education and governments.

The problem now is how best to use all this expertise to cooperate in the promotion of higher education.

CHAPTER NINE

Economic Development
The Crux of Politics

On a cold mid-November evening, more than a hundred citizens from the neighborhoods surrounding the large urban university gathered in a small auditorium in a campus building. Students going to and from classes stared at the visitors and the cadre of university administrators, including the high-profile president, who shook hands with citizens and students alike. The citizens were members of various neighborhood associations with names like the Ottawa Hillside Neighbors Association, Old Orchard Homeowners, and Secor Gardens. Although they usually met separately, the associations had asked for this joint meeting with the president through their two assigned university contacts, a young man who worked in the university's foundation and a young woman who served as dean of students. Matt reported to the vice president of government relations and Michele reported to the vice president of student affairs, both of whom were also at the meeting. Though no specific issue had upset the associations' members, there was a general desire to hear directly from the university president about his plans for the neighborhoods surrounding the campus.

The university president had made it clear, when he was told of the invitation, that although he would be happy to meet with the groups, there would have to be certain parameters, such as a time limit of one hour. He also insisted on showing, at the top of the meeting, a brief video that the university had recently produced on how the institution was managing the serious issue of campus violence. It was an appropriate gesture, since the university had dealt with a number of recent violent incidents, including the murder of a convenience store clerk within a quarter mile of university residence halls.

The president also had in mind an article by Irvin D. Reid, president emeritus of Wayne State University, in *The Presidency*, The American Council on Education's magazine for higher education leaders (fall, 2008). The article, entitled "The Urban University: Catalyst for Renewal," described Wayne State's struggles with its surrounding community during Dr. Reid's tenure as president. There are few tougher environments in America than the one Wayne State finds itself in, just west of downtown Detroit. For example, Dr. Reid wrote: "Wayne State has assumed virtually all policing around the university and some distance beyond. Local businesses no longer call the city police; they call our police department and we respond. The city has closed its own precinct near our campus."

The neighborhoods surrounding this president's university were not as challenging as the areas around Wayne State. In fact, they varied widely in their diversity. To the immediate southeast, the neighborhood was one of the poorest in the city. To the immediate northwest was one of the richest. Middle-class African-American and white neighborhoods were to the south and north, respectively. Student apartments and rentals, mixed in with residential housing, were to the east and west. The crowd in the auditorium was a mixture of young and old, homeowners and apartment owners, and African-Americans and whites.

After showing the video and talking for fifteen minutes about safety, the president opened the floor to questions. The first few questions, predictably, were about safety precautions and about student conduct off campus. There was the inevitable comment about illegal student parking along certain side streets. But then the questions shifted, in content and tone. Residents from all the various neighborhoods began asking about economic development. The questions covered all aspects of the topic from personal ("Is the university hiring?") to the universal ("What is the university's economic master plan?"). None of the neighbors brought up any fear of the university's invoking eminent domain—in fact, the president brought up the topic, and assured the crowd that the university would not take such steps. Some of the questions almost welcomed the idea of the university's expanding into the neighborhoods. One person said, "If the university is building another one of those high-tech incubator buildings, why not build it in our neighborhood so we can have some jobs?" Clearly, many of the neighbors—especially those who identified themselves as leaders of the various associations—saw the university not so much as an educational institution, but as a source of jobs and economic development.

After the meeting, which lasted a half-hour longer than the time limit that had been set, the president mingled with the audience, among them two members of the city council and three members of the city government, including the director of housing. As the president left the building and walked through the parking lot, he remarked to two of his administrators about the remarkable turn of the evening's conversation. He had expected a couple of questions about the university's role in economic development. Indeed, he had often spoken on the subject, and on the university's role in the current and future prosperity of the city, the region, and even the state. He was a member of the boards of a number of economic development groups. But here was local citizenry asking the university not just to shut down student parties by midnight but to create jobs and high-tech industries and economic leadership.

"It's a different world," the president said as he got into his car, "and we better react to it." Wayne State's Irvin Reid had said much the same thing: "A large part of an urban university's success depends on a positive relationship with visionary, inspiring, and trusted civic leadership" (p. 34).

A movement is emerging. University presidents are placing community partnerships higher on their agendas. Offices for community outreach are increasing their internal standing at colleges and universities, receiving bigger budgets and more exposure.

—From the introduction, *Beyond the Campus: How Colleges and Universities Form Partnerships with Their Communities*, by urban researcher David Maurrasse

A company called Aunt Minnie's Food, Inc., exemplifies the burden of the quote above. For about ten years Aunt Minnie—yes, there really is an Aunt Minnie, who owns the company with her daughter Claudia—has been making frozen food products that are sold in area grocery stores. She has a limited product line: sweet potato pie, peach cobbler, berry cobbler, and corn bread stuffing. They are packaged under the brand Aunt Minnie's Southern Style Entrees with the phrase "Changing the Way America Eats . . ." prominently displayed on the product's box. The company's administrative office and food production plant are in a suburb south of Toledo, Ohio. All of Aunt Minnie's employees come from neighborhoods in the vicinity of the University of Toledo.

Recently, Aunt Minnie began to have some good fortune. Or, at least it appeared to be good fortune, at first. Her product lines were picked up by a couple of major grocery chains, meaning she had to significantly (and quickly) expand her plant and workforce. Unfortunately for Aunt Minnie, the business was not automated, but rather labor intensive. The office and production plant were inexpensive in terms of rent and utilities, but the facilities could not accommodate expansion. Without capital to invest in hiring new employees, or moving to a more favorable site and expanding operations, Aunt Minnie wondered how to invest in new equipment to handle higher production volume.

She and Claudia decided to look for help. The two women learned that Louisiana officials had Katrina recovery funds to invest in companies that would agree to move to Louisiana. Although the idea of a move intrigued her, she hated the thought of abandoning her workforce and leaving her own family in Toledo. Claudia contacted Ohio's Department of Development to see if the state might provide some funding. She and Aunt Minnie also contacted their state senator—a woman they knew well. The senator was happy to initiate talks with the state's lieutenant governor, who also served at the time as the director of the Department of Development. Workforce training money might be made available. The state promised that it could and would match any offer from Louisiana or any other state.

Through the state senator, Aunt Minnie and Claudia also got in touch with a young man named Matt who coordinates real estate development for the University of Toledo. The university owned a number of off-campus buildings and a large tract of land designated as a technology park, but it could not just give Aunt Minnie's company a building or land for free. Besides, the buildings were slated to be used for scientific/technological enterprises and not for food production. Still, with Matt's help and the promise of state development funding, Aunt Minnie located an empty building that could accommodate her expanded company. Matt also introduced her to an organization that finds employment for disabled workers who could supplement the company's workforce.

What can we learn from Aunt Minnie's story? And why does the university care whether Aunt Minnie is a success, or whether she stays in the state? David Maurrasse believes it is part of the mission of a university to help the Aunt Minnies of the world. He writes "Universities and colleges are equipped to contribute effectively to their local neighborhoods in many ways, academically, economically, and beyond. For the most part, however, they are underutilized local assets" (p. 5). In other words, universities have an obligation to do the right thing.

Since this is a book about government relations and higher education, and not about ethics or urban sociology, let's examine the politics of Aunt Minnie's story.

- Aunt Minnie's Food, Inc., is an African-American-owned and operated company with a largely African-American workforce. Most of the company's employees come from neighborhoods that are adjacent to the university. The University of Toledo itself employs hundreds of minorities and has a significant African-American student population. Moral responsibility aside, it is at least practical that the university support and maintain good relations with business and political leaders of the African-American community.
- There are few things that state government despises more than companies that move out of state. The state senator and the lieutenant governor will do everything possible to make sure that Aunt Minnie stays put. The politicians will certainly be watching intently to ensure that the university does its part to help the situation. The university is smart enough to realize that if it wants state help for high-tech company development, it had better cooperate with other job development as well. After all, to the state, a job is a job, and a taxpayer is a taxpayer.
- In the same vein, the university must interface with the city of Toledo, in all sorts of ways, to pursue the development of its tech-

nology park, which happens to be the largest industrial-zoned business park within the city limits. Many issues, from infrastructure like roadways and sewers to cooperation with city economic planners, are involved. The university must hire employees like Matt full time to keep on top of the city relationship. Shunning the needs of Aunt Minnie would not please city planners, politicians, or citizens.

The university felt significant political pressure from state and local officials to address the needs of Aunt Minnie's Foods, Inc., as well as paying heed to personal lobbying from Aunt Minnie, her daughter, and leaders of the African-American community. Still, one might ask, what does economic development have to do with the true mission of a university—to educate students? Or is that no longer the university's only mission? This is a complicated and evolving question, one that engages many segments of the university community, including faculty. The question is important enough to warrant some historical perspective.

Not so long ago, the student bodies of universities and colleges were divided into two groups. One group of students took classes for the love of learning. Many did not know or even care what they were going to do after graduation. When they graduated, the university president would hand them diplomas and wave them good-bye. The second group of students, composed mostly of education majors, was training to become teachers. This training involved a type of internship called student teaching. Unlike their friends in the first group, education majors knew exactly what they were going to do after graduation.

I understand that this is a gross generalization. Many students who were not going to be teachers nonetheless knew what they were going to do after college. They were getting an education to take over the family business, or to become an accountant or a scientist, because that is what they always wanted to be. Some disciplines—notably engineering and medicine—always offered internships to provide students with specific training. Nevertheless, it is true that most areas of most universities did not particularly care what their graduates did after graduation day.

Today, things are very different. Most students will be doing internships in their chosen fields. Many demand internship opportunities, because they know the importance of hands-on training. Students today expect to step out of the university and into a good-paying job. And they expect their universities to facilitate that transition in as many ways as possible. To accomplish this, universities have had to re-engineer their practices to become more involved in economic development.

- Universities are home to any number of institutes and centers that deal with economic development. These include such diverse areas as urban affairs, small businesses, transportation, and economic roundtables. Most of these centers—except for some of those in colleges of business—were established primarily as research and study centers. Business centers present more of an entrepreneurial aspect, in terms of providing business faculty a mechanism for consulting. All of these centers are adept at publishing monographs and reports, but overall do very little teaching.

- Universities have created technology parks or technology corridors. One of the oldest and most famous of these, of course, is the Research Triangle in North Carolina, involving Duke University, North Carolina State University, and the University of North Carolina. Other notable high-tech corridors were created around Boston and in Silicon Valley, and many larger universities have emulated these models. Some of these corridors have succeeded and some have failed. But in every case, universities and/or university foundations found themselves investing significant funds in technology park development, hoping to lure the next Microsoft or Google to a university-owned facility.

- Universities recognized that adult learners were a new source of students, although the adult student is primarily motivated to learn practical job skills in order to advance in the workforce. This realization forced significant changes in university curricula, and encouraged the development of distance learning as a viable education tool.

- University researchers discovered that much of the research funding that came from their states or came from congressional earmarks was often economically oriented. Funding came with the proviso that the results have a practical and applicable aspect— meaning the creation of businesses, products, and jobs. Universities scrambled to enact patent policies and agreements that would allow researchers to share in research success.

- Universities have increasingly found themselves being used by city, county, state, and federal governments as conduits for workforce training and economic development. Sometimes the university just functions as a convenient pass-through entity. Often, however, at least part of the funding involves some sort of educational training. This money is usually unbudgeted "found" money that is hard for universities to pass up.

- Universities—often under pressure from regents and legislators— have altered many of their courses of study to emphasize real-world aspects of traditional disciplines. The idea is that this type of "training" will lead to jobs.

Notice, ironically, that not one of these six points fits what the University of Toledo did for Aunt Minnie's Food, Inc. But the university could have helped in traditional ways. It could have asked one of its business professors to give Aunt Minnie some marketing advice. It could have provided land for, or offered to build, a food processing plant in its own technology park. Perhaps the university could have funneled some state workforce training money to the training of Aunt Minnie's employees on new automated equipment. Someday, the university may do one or maybe all of these things. Making that determination is the moment when government relations becomes important.

A good office of government relations and good government relations officers are essential for all university economic development initiatives. The problem that universities had, before the rise of government relations as a viable administrative office, was that no one coordinated economic development efforts. It was not that good work was not being done—it was. But it was done in isolation, and few were looking at the big picture. Presidents and provosts, who were in a position to see the big picture, were often overworked and embattled by traditional administrative concerns within the university's walls. Until government relations people came along, no one was conveying effectively the economic needs of government to the campus. Some researchers caught on, but only in terms of their research. Some continuing education/adult learning offices caught on, but only in terms of workforce training. Some business professors caught on, but only in terms of their own consulting.

Government relations offices have been able to pull these disparate constituencies together, and to coordinate efforts. Universities that do have government relations officers benefit from better coordination among participating areas, lower administrative overhead, economic development opportunities, and, perhaps most important, recognition from the university's surrounding community and governments that the university cares about progress and the future.

This last point must not be taken lightly. Good will is hard to measure. Suffice it to say that universities have traditionally had a negative attitude toward "townies." Contributions to economic development have given institutions of higher education an unprecedented opportunity to repair those old attitudes, and to become economic leaders in their community as well as education leaders.

Ohio's Board of Regents recently issued the following statement, as one of its four mission goals: "The University System will provide the intellectual and organizational infrastructure to measurably improve the economic outlook for all the citizens of the state." This statement, which falls under the title "Economic Leadership," carries as much weight as the document's other three mission goals of "Access," "Quality of Teaching," and "Affordability."

In pursuing this economic leadership mission, the regents have partnered with Ohio's Department of Development to promote economic development. For example, a new program divides the state into twelve regions, and in each region pairs a Department of Development job director with a Board of Regents education coordinator. The idea is that the regional job director will line up new businesses—either start-ups or businesses enticed from other states—and the education coordinator will then arrange for the new business's workforce and coordinate such job training as may be needed.

On many levels, this is a viable idea. It should be apparent, however, that public community colleges and universities are being dragged into economic development, whether or not they want to be. Of course, every institution wants to be, and the state and the regents offer a number of financial incentives for participation. And the regents' mission statement (quoted above) states that higher education will "improve the economic outlook for all citizens." Higher education in Ohio no longer has a choice; it has an obligation.

But how exactly have we arrived at this state of affairs? Richard M. Rosan of the Urban Land Institute has written: "Few institutions have more to offer in propelling economic development on both a national and local basis than our nations' colleges and Universities. As leading institutions in their communities, they are powerful drivers, technology centers, employers, developers and investors." All true: universities have it all and do it all. But for decades, universities were satisfied merely to be—for want of a better phrase—a large lump on a log. Or perhaps a bloated frog, croaking and snatching the occasional fly that flew too close. In other words, higher education contributed to the economy just by being. Occasionally, to show how important it was, a university would issue an "economic impact" study. Most of these studies are the same. Even small institutions claim to turn over hundreds of thousands of dollars to the local community, in terms of employee salaries and purchase of local services. Faculty members buy houses and students rent apartments. Local contractors build campus buildings. The beverage distributor supplies vending machines with soda and snacks. Universities even take credit for community entertainment, whether it is athletics or theater productions.

Much of this activity is passive. In the end, universities exist for themselves and not for the betterment of their communities, regions, or states. Economically speaking, universities exist in a top-down circumstance, not a bottom-up environment. What exactly does that mean?

Eva Klein, a Washington consultant specializing in higher education and economic development, helps universities adapt to what she calls "integrated knowledge communities." She says on her Web site (www .evakleinassociates.com) that "Universities and colleges are principal regional assets for economic transformation and growth. Higher education institutions develop and commercialize new technologies, provide the skilled knowledge workforce at all levels, support business formation and growth, represent major forces in community development, and form a large part of a community's quality of life." She maintains that "universities have to be the decision place." In other words, universities do not dictate economic development by, say, signing an agreement with the local Coca-Cola distributor. Instead, universities provide the basis for future economic growth with the land, know-how, and willingness to engage companies and developers in efforts to start businesses, hire employees, and grow the local economy.

Eugene P. Trani, Virginia Commonwealth University president emeritus, in the May 16, 2008, issue of the *Chronicle of Higher Education,* writes: "The connections between universities and our communities are essential to our core functions and are increasingly vital to our continuing success as well as the long-term prosperity of the nation's cities, regions, and states." President Trani would no doubt support Ohio's higher education mission, which equated Ohio's welfare and prosperity with economic development fueled by the state's higher education system. He adds: "As the knowledge economy becomes more sophisticated, the country's towns, cities, and regions need more of everything that universities have to offer . . . . Put simply, universities are becoming indispensable partners in almost every major activity in which society is engaged."

Professor Neil Reid of the University of Toledo's Urban Affairs Center has written about another important way in which universities participate in economic development. His research has centered on a concept popularly known as an economic development cluster. Dr. Reid writes:

A cluster-based economic development strategy works most effectively when businesses in a particular industry in a particular geographic region collaborate with the university and other community partners to develop a collective vision for the future competitiveness of the industry and then collaborate strategically to implement that vision. Institutions of higher education are a key partner in any successful cluster-based economic development strategy. Universities can contribute in a number of important ways. First, they can work with the local industry to ensure that their curriculum is tailored to meet the needs of the industry. Second, they can work with the local industry to ensure that their research programs, particularly in science and engineering, are aligned to the needs of the industry. Third, they can work with local industry to provide assessment and analysis of

local business conditions, current and future market trends, and best practices in local economic development.

Reid says that the cluster strategy has been especially successful in
foreign settings, such as the United Kingdom, where an aging industrial
base has needed technological assistance from higher education.

In summary, most universities have torn down (or are tearing down)
the walls that once surrounded institutions of higher education. Higher
education is lowering access barriers not only for students, but also for
the community at large. Theories of how to create these integrated knowledge communities are fine and useful, but the challenge is for universities to figure out how to accomplish this task.

If economic development is indeed the future of higher education, why
do so few university faculty, staff, and students know about it? Why isn't
economic development a stated mission at most universities? When a
university does become involved in economic development, why doesn't
it more prominently promote that involvement to the public?

The answers to these questions vary in relation to where the university
is located and exactly what the university wants to accomplish. For example,
what if neighborhood development is not an issue? Certainly, many established universities are located in older urban neighborhoods. Some
institutions—such as Wayne State University—are in economically dis-
tressed areas of cities. To their credit, many of these universities have
sought to revitalize and develop their surrounding neighborhoods. But
what is the moral responsibility if the "bad" neighborhood is miles away,
clear on the other side of the city from the university? Does the university
still have an obligation to rehab that neighborhood and establish workforce training programs for that neighborhood's residents?

Another challenge is the manpower and money a university can devote to economic development. Economic development is a labor-intensive
job. Helping a start-up company, for example, involves thousands of details and decisions. The process takes months, if not years. If a university
government relations officer gets caught up in just a few such projects,

the effort will probably suck away most of her time, time that could—and probably should—be spent on other projects.

Economic development is a challenge for a university if it runs afoul of a long-standing liberal arts tradition at the institution. A school that prides itself on teaching and scholarship (and what school doesn't?) may have faculty and administrators who believe that throwing money at economic development projects is just wasting resources that could be used to support teaching and scholarship. How does a university achieve an appropriate balance?

What about those finances? Some universities lack budgets that would allow discretionary funds for economic development, and may choose to tap their foundation money. But truthfully, few foundations and their boards—who traditionally like to give out scholarships and research grants—are very excited about spending money on risky start-up businesses or technology parks. So if resources are limited, what can a university do? Is upgrading a surrounding neighborhood more important than building a new science laboratory, or offering more student scholarships?

And, of course, the university's governing body may not be willing to see the university adopt an economic development mission. Trustees may believe first in good old-fashioned education, not in entrepreneurial globalization.

Finally, governments that generally enjoy having university involvement and resources are sometimes so bureaucratic that they simply cannot get their arms around university efforts. In other words, some governments are not very flexible or adaptable to progressive economic development ideas that universities may suggest. A few years ago, Ohio's eighty-eight county governments were holding hundreds of millions of dollars of federal workforce training funds. Some large urban counties gave money to agencies for workforce training, but the vast majority of counties had no such agencies, and in effect no mechanism to distribute the training funds. The governor tried to reclaim the funds, with the idea of distributing the money to public community colleges and universities that were equipped to do training. The counties, however, resisted the governor's efforts, and he managed to wrestle away only about $30 million, which was distributed to higher education. To this day, there are still hundreds of millions of dollars sitting in restricted county accounts across the state. Bureaucracy triumphs!

The message of the preceding paragraph is at the heart of the great bureaucratic tangle created by the stimulus funding from the American Recovery and Reinvestment Act of 2009. So much money, involving so many government agencies on both the giving and the receiving ends, that had to be spent in so little time.

A university's government relations officer seeking to engage in economic development faces many obstacles, no matter how hard he or she is lobbied to assist city/county governments, state government, or even the federal government, to spend money and help people. That is the ultimate challenge for government relations officers. A government relations officer must use the art of negotiation. He or she must balance politics and ideology. He or she must be able to argue that the future benefits of economic development are as important to the university as investing in a new science building. Government relations is not easy. It is a challenge.

CHAPTER TEN

Interviews with Higher Education Government Relations Professionals

What follows are interviews with three government relations officers who work at three Midwestern public universities. I chose these three—two of whom I have known for a number of years—not because of their institutions, but because they all view themselves as government relations professionals and would identify themselves as working in local, state, and national politics. In other words, they do not view themselves as doing primarily a separate administrative job, with government relations as a sidelight or afterthought. I am indebted to the three of them for their candor, and for taking the time from their busy schedules to sit down with me and discuss the profession of government relations in higher education.

MARGIE ROLF, ASSISTANT VICE PRESIDENT FOR GOVERNMENTAL RELATIONS, THE UNIVERSITY OF CINCINNATI

Question: How did you become involved in working with government relations?

Answer: I became involved in government relations because my parents were involved in politics. It really was just second nature for me when I grew up. I immediately felt at home with politics, and I really can't imagine doing anything else. For me it's just a natural way of life. My father was first elected to the Ohio state senate in 1972 and served there until 1985. He ran for governor of Ohio in 1985, losing in the Republican primary election. Later, he served one term in the Ohio house of representatives before starting a governmental affairs consulting firm. He passed away in 1992 at the early age of 48, but not before instilling in me the love of politics and the responsibility of serving in my community.

Very early in my life, my father would take me to political meetings, or along with him when he was campaigning. He worked hard to serve his district and to assist his colleagues in the senate, so he was generally gone traveling the state during the week. Our way of spending time together was by going to various political events on the weekends, when it didn't interrupt my schooling. This included attending dinners, radio interviews, and participating in parades. I also recall watching him talking on the phone with a legal pad in hand, trying to redistrict the legislative maps of Ohio. Obviously, this was well before computers. But from all of this, I was able to learn about my state and the people in it—their needs and desires as well as their hopes and dreams.

Question: Since you live and work in Columbus, what are the advantages and disadvantages of being a hundred miles away from the University of Cincinnati campus?

Answer: Well, in my position, here I am the eyes and ears of the university at the state level. We have additional staff members who represent the university at the federal and local level, but in Columbus, I am the campus identity for legislators and the administration. To assist with this identity, I wear the school colors—red and black—as much as possible. There are advantages and disadvantages of being located both on campus and remotely. The most obvious disadvantage to not being on campus is not being able to feed off of the energy that the students generate. I try to compensate for this by maintaining a close relationship with our student government leaders, whom I enjoy working with tremendously. The advantage to working at the statehouse [is that it] allows me to be extremely focused on governmental relations efforts and to be able to put the university in a position to have better intelligence than they might not otherwise have. This is not to say that I don't ever come to campus. It is important that I meet with our people face-to-face at times, to really talk through an issue or develop an important relationship (campus relationships are just as important as those at the statehouse). Therefore, I tend to go to campus about once a month for various meetings and events.

Question: Describe your typical day at the state capitol.

Answer: Every day is different, which is part of what I enjoy most about my job. When the legislature is in session, my schedule is dictated more by their calendar, which includes meeting with members or their staff, attending committee hearings, and providing input on issues being debated as appropriate on behalf of the university. When the legislature is out of session, my schedule is filled with discussing issues with legislators and their staffs and attending to any constituent work that they may forward to me. Additionally, I spend a great deal of time researching and developing issues to forward before the legislature or the administration.

Question: How do you coordinate your state efforts with what the university is doing at home with city and county governments and in Washington at the federal level?

Answer: It's a team effort, and we utilize the 2Cs—communication and coordination—at every step. My boss, the vice president for communications and government relations, takes care of a lot of the local politics, as he is based on campus. Then we have a lobbying firm that we use in Washington for the federal arena. We have standing conference calls with one another, to provide updates and status checks and also to talk through issues. Additionally, for the past few years, we have developed an annual strategic plan for government relations that helps keep us focused and coordinated, and has proven to be an effective tool.

Question: Can you give me an example of all three government entities working together?

Answer: A great example is the UC Cancer Center. Ohio is in the unique and unenviable position of having a moderate incidence of cancer and a disproportionately high cancer-related death rate. Despite the fact that Ohio had the twenty-fifth highest cancer incidence of forty-six states reporting for the period 1999 to 2003, Ohioans had the twelfth highest cancer death rate of all fifty states for that period. This places Ohio in the top 25 percent of cancer death rates by state.

In order to alleviate this disturbing problem, the University of Cincinnati has formed a joint cancer program with our local partners—the University Hospital and Cincinnati Children's Hospital Medical Center—to be the catalyst for bringing state-of-the-art cancer care to the people of southwestern Ohio. Our ultimate goal in this endeavor is to achieve NCI designation as a Cancer Center, in order to ensure that our underserved minority and Appalachian populations receive the cancer prevention and treatment programs they so desperately need.

We have been working within our community to gain support for this effort, while at the same time working at the state level to gain funding to upgrade our facilities and capabilities, and then at the federal level working through the NCI requirements to receive such a designation. It is actually a very exciting opportunity, and one that can have such an enormous impact on our community for many years to come.

Question: Can you pick up the phone and directly call your president? [The president at the time of the interview was Nancy L. Zimpher. Dr. Zimpher is now chancellor of SUNY.]
Answer: Yes, but it's hard to get her on the phone. I've never seen someone keep a calendar the way she does! It's easier to communicate with her through e-mail. I've found that no matter what part of the world she is in, she is always tuned into her e-mail for a part of the day. Also, I can go to any member of the senior leadership team that I need to speak with about an issue.

Question: What's the most difficult aspect of working with state legislators?
Answer: I think it's getting legislators' attention on certain issues—and sometimes getting less attention on others. They are busy people and with a lot of people and issues asking for their attention—it's just hard sometimes to get them to focus on the university's needs. Many legislators tend to know higher education issues only through their own experience in college or perhaps [that of] a son or daughter. Depending upon their own experience, and how recent, [that] can greatly influence how a topic should be broached with that member. For instance, while in Ohio campus housing is an auxiliary function with no state support, there seems to be an annual conversation about how "lavish" the dormitories can be for our students. It can be challenging to explain to a legislator the wants and desires in student housing today—by not only the student but also the parent—when the last time they stepped foot in a dorm room was

in 1964. Students' and parents' attitudes and expectations have changed a great deal from what they experienced.

Question: Who's harder to deal with: Republicans or Democrats?
Answer: It's not a matter of party affiliation—rather, it's really more about finding the members who are willing to invest the time and effort into an issue.

Question: How often do you go to state agencies, including the Ohio Board of Regents? What are examples of some higher education issues involving agencies?
Answer: I work most often with the board of regents—our coordinating board. Our relationship is mostly congenial. We are in the process of changing the structure in Ohio's higher education system—and that is a system with a small "s"! This is relatively new territory for all of us, and on both sides of the equation with procedures being changed and in some cases, the way we conduct business. It can be confusing at times, so it requires a very regular contact with key staff and the chancellor to ensure that miscommunication and unintended consequences can be kept to a minimum.

I also work from time to time with other state agencies—the Department of Development being the largest. Because of the recognition by the current administration that education—and especially higher education and degree attainment—is the key to economic prosperity, the department is reaching out to universities more and more in seeking ways to attract new businesses to Ohio and provide support to those currently here. The best example of this with my institution is that the administration recently was successful in having a pharmaceutical company relocate near to my campus. Working together, we brought appropriate personnel from the university to the table to discuss the possibility of starting a new degree program that would benefit the company and other workforce development tools. These efforts by the University of Cincinnati played a big role in making the determination for the company's relocation.

Question: Does the governor get involved often?
Answer: The governor has shown a great deal of interest and support in higher education to date. This support has ranged from additional finan-

cial support to providing new opportunities for new programs and grants. The governor certainly understands our value to turning the Ohio economy in the right direction, so he tends to involve himself more in this arena. But he has drawn the line at getting involved in any day-to-day activities or those matters best left to either the [university's] president or board of trustees.

Question: Would you recommend government relations as a profession? What do you really want to do when you grow up?

Answer: I have often thought about what if I wasn't doing what I'm doing, what would I do instead? And while I have considered taking different paths, I have always come home to government relations. It was what I am supposed to do as my profession. When I really grow up, I want to be a good mom to my two kids and enjoy my family. And, hopefully by doing what I do now, I will have instilled in them a love and responsibility for their community by example.

RICHARD LEWIS, DIRECTOR OF GOVERNMENTAL
RELATIONS, NORTHEASTERN OHIO UNIVERSITIES
COLLEGES OF MEDICINE AND PHARMACY

Question: One of the points I make in the book is about the importance of mentors. Did you have a mentor, and how did that affect where you ended up?

Answer: I have had a couple of mentors over the years, one who helped me as a program designer and educator and administrator, and another who helped me in terms of interacting with folks in Washington. The importance of the role both have played is that none of what we do with elected officials is very complicated—it is not rocket science. The hard part is not in figuring it out or how to develop and present a program or idea. The hard part is figuring out how to convince others to support your proposal, so that their decisions work in the best interests of your programs and your institution.

The primary [factor in] why I became involved in legislative affairs [was] a small grant I had in 1974, when I was finishing up my graduate degrees. I realized very quickly that if I wanted to get my next grant, I was going to have to develop the idea, write it up, and then market it to the folks who had funding to support it. In that particular case, it was a group called the Regional Medical Programs out of Lexington, Kentucky. So that was my first introduction to program funding and politics, which then led to my work in Washington and eventually, my work in Columbus to develop the relationships and the contacts needed to identify funding sources to get my next set of grants.

Question: Describe NEOUCOM a little bit, and the fact that you're the only person there having to do everything in government relations.

Answer: The Northeastern Ohio Universities Colleges of Medicine and Pharmacy enrolls an average of 115 medical students each year in the BS/MD program. Our students start immediately after high school and attend their first two years of college at one of three universities: Youngstown State University, Kent State University, and the University of Akron. Soon we will be adding 35 students through Cleveland State University. We will eventually average 150 students per class for a total of 600 medical students.

After two to three years on one of the university campuses, these students come to the NEOUCOM campus to attend medical college classes. At the end of as few as six years, they are able to graduate with a baccalaureate degree from one of the originating universities and a medical degree from NEOUCOM. Essentially, in six years, they accumulate the same number of hours as they would have if they had attended eight years of college, due in part to attending classes throughout the year.

The pharmacy program is a doctorate in pharmacy, Pharm.D, and we accept 75 students per year. Those students participate in what we call a "2 + 4" program. We call it that because they will spend the first two years at one of our partner university campuses in pre-pharmacy courses such as English, math, history, social studies, biological sciences, chemistry, and physics. Then if their grades and test scores meet our admissions criteria, they come forward to the College of Pharmacy for four years in the Pharm.D. program. After six years, they can graduate with one degree, a doctor of pharmacy degree (Pharm.D.).

Two other unique aspects of NEOUCOM are that we are one of the very few remaining independent medical colleges in the country, and we may be the only institution which is training pharmacy students and medical students in an interdisciplinary curriculum, together, at the same time, in the same classroom, for a significant portion of their education.

Regarding my role as the individual who conducts all the government relations, that is historical, and it started from day one when I was hired to serve as vice president for administration and public relations in 1983. During the first six months of my tenure, I asked several senior staff and faculty members the question: "How does NEOUCOM obtain funds from the state?" The response was: "Well, we go through the University of Akron and they help us take care of that." And I said, "Well, what about capital construction funding?" and the response was: "The University of Akron decides what we need." And, after picking myself up off the floor, I answered, "Not anymore; we're going to change that approach and pursue our own priorities and funding streams!"

I started on July 1, 1983, and over Christmas break, December of 1983, I wrote three capital project proposals for funding that would come directly to NEOUCOM. I presented them to our board of trustees for approval, and then submitted them to the Ohio Board of Regents, who approved one of the three programs. The other two programs, along with the approved program, I then presented directly to the state legislature, and got the legislature to approve the other two. So, in essence, the legislature approved all three, with the support of the regents on one of them, for a total appropriation to NEOUCOM of $7.1 million in 1984.

And that was the beginning of my major role in identifying funding sources and then pursuing project funding. I became the project designer, funds obtainer, project developer, and project completer, and then once it was completed, I administered the facilities.

Question: But a principle arises from that, and that is that the value of government relations is that it means you're taking care of your institution and not letting someone else dictate how it's being taken care of.

Answer: Correct. In terms of everything from responding to government regulations and legislation that would affect our institution, to capital funding, to operational funding. I have been convinced, from day one, that a person hired by the president, and who reports directly to the president, is the one most appropriate to serve that need. My view is based on my assumption that that employee would have a working knowledge of the organization, knowledge of academics, and knowledge, in our case, of biomedical sciences research and medical and pharmacy education.

I also believe that loyalty to the institution is tied directly to being an employee of that institution. For someone in my position who is an internal government relations person, there is never any doubt about whom I work for, whom I represent, and what my loyalties are. My institution can count on that. The Ohio General Assembly can count on that. The Ohio Board of Regents, the governor, and the Ohio congressional delegation can all count on the fact that when I walk in to talk with them about an issue, they know whom I represent.

Question: Now, in that list you left out your immediate community, your city, and your county government. Do you take care of that, or is that not an issue in your particular institution?

Answer: I do work closely with county governments in Akron, Canton, and Youngstown, and soon we may be doing some things in Cleveland. That is an enormous task, one that eventually will require someone to focus specifically on that area.

Question: How do city government and county government in a city miles away affect a specialized school?

Answer: We actually have numerous campuses. Our primary basic medical sciences campus and administrative campus is in Rootstown, which is centrally located in our geographic region. We're within 45 minutes of Cleveland, Akron, Canton, and Youngstown. We're within 45 minutes of 40 percent of the state's population. However, we have, as part of our mission, assumed a responsibility to increase our presence in Akron and Cleveland initially, and also to work with Canton and Youngstown to increase our presence in those communities. That means that we are trying to develop significant academic and research projects with physicians, the teaching hospitals, and the universities in those communities to enhance our funding, to enhance our opportunities, and to strengthen our long-term future.

Question: But that sounds like an academic project, not a city/county government project.

Answer: Using Akron as an example: The mayor of the city of Akron has developed a very forward-thinking approach to redesigning the downtown Akron area. He has identified and mapped out what is called the "Akron Biomedical Corridor" which now includes land occupied by the University of Akron, Summa Health System, Akron General Medical Center, and Akron Children's Hospital, as well as land that links and is contiguous to these institutions.

All of our medical students are educated through Akron Children's Hospital Pediatrics, and on average, a majority of our students rotate through Akron General Medical Center and Summa Health System. When the Biomedical Corridor was created, we met with the mayor of Akron, who agreed that NEOUCOM should be a party to this biomedical corridor. Its purpose is to revitalize the economy of the city and to enhance approaches that would bring all five universities and hospital partners together, including NEOUCOM, to promote economic development and research.

We are hopeful that we can do something similar in Canton and in Youngstown, and we've initiated those conversations. The city of Cleveland has been doing this for years in terms of developing a corridor that has pretty much linked downtown Cleveland to the Cleveland Clinic, to the University Hospital System, Rainbow Babies & Children's Hospital, and to Case Western Reserve University, to serve as one very large economic engine that has contributed positively to the economic growth of the city of Cleveland.

Question: Changing the topic, would you agree with the premise that at the federal level your presence is necessary, but that you can't really affect much? Or can you affect getting funds or changing policy?

Answer: In general, I would agree with that. For someone like me to have a significant impact in Washington would mean spending an enormous amount of time there. I will never have the time nor the financial resources to be able to do so. My reference to financial resources means travel money. Not other types of money. Because I have other responsibilities, and many people like me also have other responsibilities which limit our ability to be two places at once. My ability, in general, to impact what's going on in Washington is facilitated through the Association of American Medical Colleges, the American Council on Education, the National Association of State Universities and Land-Grant Colleges, the American Medical Association, the American Academy of Family Practice, the Council on Teaching Hospitals, and many others.

So, I work closely with the legislative staff from those organizations as well as congressional staff members, to attempt to impact significant issues which are coming our way. It is very difficult, but in a general way by combining our efforts with many others, we can help influence issues. In terms of addressing institution-specific issues, if I am asked by my president and/or my board to represent our interests, I do so on a regular basis. My efforts and communications focus on members of the Ohio congressional delegation in general, and specifically on those members from northeast Ohio.

Another approach that I have used successfully is to combine my legislative efforts with those of another institution to develop and present a project that each institution's delegation could support, and from which both of us could benefit.

Question: Final question. How has the profession of government relations changed in your nearly thirty-five years of doing this?
Answer: Fewer individuals who have grown out of the academic or university setting are getting involved in government relations. It appears that many of the younger people who are now involved in government relations started out on the political side, first as staff members to state representatives or senators, and then were hired by colleges and universities to represent them.

Where there is a shortfall among some individuals who represent colleges and universities is that they have not had experience or a working knowledge of the challenges that comes with serving as a university administrator or running an academic program. In my case, my experiences were based initially on developing educational programs. My involvement in politics grew out of that knowledge base. I developed an understanding of the political process, communications, and relationship-building out of the necessity to obtain funding for my programmatic efforts. Whereas a sizeable group of the folks now coming into government relations have to learn about the nuances of the academic side, and it can be very difficult because administering a university and teaching students is foreign to many people. That's one piece.

The other piece has to do with hiring outside lobbyists to work for public higher education. I personally am opposed to the retention of contract lobbyists. I think it is a concern from the standpoint that if an institution has a contract lobbyist, that contract lobbyist's ability to make a living normally requires having more than one client and often, seven, eight, nine, or ten clients. So, when push comes to shove in a budget hearing, or in the budget process, or in a conference committee, and there are several amendments that need to be pressed forward, that person could well be put into a position by a legislator who says, "Okay, you have three/four amendments here, you're only going to get one, which one do you want me to put into this bill?" My view is that the contract lobbyist will defer to the group that's paying him/her the most money, which may or may not be the university which has retained him/her. In situations such as this, you can never be certain where that lobbyist's loyalties lie.

CYNTHIA WILBANKS, VICE PRESIDENT FOR GOVERNMENT
RELATIONS, THE UNIVERSITY OF MICHIGAN

Question: How did you get into government relations? I've written elsewhere in this book about the value of having mentors, and wonder if you had any.

Answer: I actually came into a government relations role with the university from a twenty-year career working in the federal government. I worked for two members of Congress who represented the Ann Arbor region. Our main district office, for both members, was located in Ann Arbor, and it was a wonderful platform from which to get acquainted with the community and be much more involved with the University of Michigan. The university was part of my beat, as I used to call it. It gave me a chance to interact with the leadership of the institution over that period, which was an extraordinary way to become familiar, not only with the leaders of the institution, but also many faculty, many staff, and students over those years. That career really then came to a close when my boss retired after sixteen years. He had been a member of the Appropriations Committee, so we had frequent contacts with folks at the university about federal funding for research, student aid, and higher education policy issues. I spent the next couple of years heading up a child advocacy organization in the state, but then was called to consider a couple of positions at the University of Michigan, one of which was an associate vice president for state relations. During that time, the university was organized a little differently. The administrative umbrella was called university relations, and it included federal relations, state relations, and public affairs. The arrangement was not that unusual in the mid-1990s.

So, from a career path in government, I made the transition to the University of Michigan. I like to say that I simply moved from one side of the desk to the other. There is no doubt, however, that the opportunity to work on the government side was a valuable asset. I'm a University of Michigan graduate, so that affinity never really leaves you, and it was a real honor for me to come to the university in a government relations position.

You asked about a mentor. I'm not sure that I had a mentor in the traditional sense of having someone who helps guide your career, provides advice, or acts as a sounding board. But, I was familiar with one of the longest-serving members of the university leadership team, who also served in the role of vice president for government relations and university relations, as well as secretary of the board. I knew him for many, many years and always admired his work. I observed, and I was fully aware of the kind of work that he did and found it remarkable that he stayed on a pretty even keel, even in turbulent times. Even from those observations and the interactions that we did have, while not in a traditional mentor role, I think he served as model. Even though I was well into my career, it never hurts to have somebody that you can refer back to.

Question: You mentioned that when you started, or were looking at employment at the University of Michigan, it was a different organizational structure. Can you talk about the organization now?

Answer: When I came, as I said, I was under the university relations umbrella, and my boss at the time held the title of vice president for university relations. My observation was that his plate was full. I was expected to report to him on various issues. But he gave me free reign. He was not at all reluctant to suggest that I could have complete access to the president, directly, without going through him. But in fact it was a structure, and I respect the structure, hierarchy, and process that characterize most large and complex organizations. Nonetheless, when my boss went on to be a president of another university, I went to the new president of the university and said, "I want to share with you two thoughts. One, after working here for three years under this type of an organizational structure, I would strongly recommend you separate the communications function from the government relations function. We have enormous communication challenges here. The public affairs division here can consume you. It ties you to your desk. I just don't think a vice president for university relations can really adequately meet all of the objectives in that kind of a role when the public affairs function is so time-consuming, and I thought it would be a useful opportunity to at least take a look at separating government relations from the public affairs function."

The second thing I said was, "If you make a decision along that line to restructure, I would be very interested in assuming the role of vice president for government relations, as I think my background and experience would at least warrant consideration for that post." And on both counts, he agreed, and as a result I've been vice president for government relations for ten years at the University of Michigan.

Question: Talking about your structure, though—just a small point, but I thought it was interesting—why does government relations manage the university's United Way campaign?

Answer: Well, it is a function, an extension, if you will, of our community relations profile. As we know, United Way organizations have succeeded through the years by working with large employers in their communities to maximize participation in their yearly fund-raising activities. The University of Michigan is the largest employer in our area, and we have had a long-standing affiliation with the Washtenaw County United Way. We identify university leaders for our campaign effort and organize the mechanics of running the campaign, sending materials to our employees, and conducting various campaign activities to support the overall United Way fund-raising goals. I believe it is very important for the university to be viewed as a community partner in the work of providing health, education, and social services to our greater community. I don't think you can separate the community's well-being from the university's well-being, and one way to support the community's well-being is through the United Way.

Question: Can you make a leap, because this sounds a lot like if I had asked the question about economic development instead of the United Way, you might have gone down a similar path.

Answer: Sure. Economic development is another area where we have taken major steps to increase our commitment, our visibility, and our involvement in extending the university's resources to support regional and statewide activity. We have the highest levels of the university's leadership committed to a partner role in the region and in the community, to advance economic development goals.

Presidential leadership in this area really matters—and I think it's fair to say that major research universities in particular have become much more attentive to supporting and expanding our footprint in economic development initiatives. We now have a president who is entering her seventh year, who has clearly and consistently articulated the university's relevance to an economic development agenda, and has made some strategic hires to stimulate these partnerships. Our vice president for research is a clear example of such a hire; he is an active partner and collaborator with other organizations in our community, in the state, and among other universities in a variety of economic development initiatives. In addition, we are dedicating financial resources to support these efforts. I view these activities as very strategic and smart, since the university's long-term well-being as a publicly supported institution is so dependent on a strong state economy.

Question: Doesn't that take all of your staff time to coordinate it?

Answer: In addition to my government relations role, I also advise the president on various economic development activities/initiatives that are going on around the state. The vice president of research and I work very closely together with regard to many of these activities, and we are eager to look at opportunities where the university's role and specific expertise can be most helpful and can be leveraged to the best and highest benefits.

Could I spend a lot of time on economic development—like every waking minute of every hour? Sure. But I am comfortable with the framework that we've established in order to accomplish those goals, and we have many more people now at the university who are a phone call away from local, regional, and state economic development officials. That responsiveness, more than anything else, is what has been so important to achieve. And when you're on the outside trying to get into a large organization, the front door can be difficult to find, and even more difficult to penetrate. It can be very intimidating for many people and businesses, extraordinarily frustrating. So we've done some work here to streamline that opportunity to get in a front door and fully leverage, where possible, the university's resources with the goals of the community.

Question: Speaking of the vice president for research, how do you handle Washington then?

Answer: The University of Michigan has really been a pioneer in the federal relations arena. Back when I was working in the congressional offices, we had routine communications and visits from people who were ambassadors from campus to Washington. It was pretty typical for officials to travel to Washington three, four, five days a month to pursue federal research opportunities and to advocate for the university's interests.

By 1990, after very serious discussion and consultation, a decision was reached to establish a permanent office in Washington, D.C. The model called for the office to be staffed with individuals working both Capitol Hill and in the various executive departments, as well as in the expectation that they would be collaborating and working hand in hand with higher education associations like the AAU, NASULGC, and ACE.

At the time, the move was viewed as pretty gutsy. Most took a wait-and-see attitude, not quite sure how it would work out. However, over nearly twenty years, many institutions have followed suit and have found a Washington presence similar to ours in structure to be very, very useful. And I can't say enough about the ways in which that team is on the ground with not only the members of Congress, but, as importantly, their staffs, on a regular basis to communicate, not only on behalf of the university, but also on behalf of higher education institutions more broadly.

We were a pioneer. I think at the time, there might have been less than half a dozen schools and colleges with a permanent presence in Washington of that kind, and today it's proliferated to many, many more.

Question: Do you have free and easy access to the university's president?
Answer: Absolutely! I'm not sure you can really do this work without having frequent access. When I got the call from the president and he said, "Okay, you've got the job," I was, of course, elated. But I had to call back, and I said, "I forgot to say a few other things. One, keep in mind that my philosophy in doing this job is that I have to be outside of the office all or most of the time. If my light is on, I'm not really doing the job that I think this position requires. So, I'm not coming to all your meetings. I am not going to be at every event in the evening, even though, being a member of the executive officer team, we're expected to be at some of these events. Please keep that in mind. I just can't do this job directing others to do it." He said, "I got it!" Then I said: "Second, I am not going to darken your door for every little thing. I'll let you know when I think something is important. Otherwise, I expect that you know that I'm going to do what I think is best." He said, "Yep, got that, too!" Having said that, I just can't say enough about the immediate access that I did have and I continue to have.

Question: You have the president's cell phone number?
Answer: I do. If I have to call at 11:30 at night or at 1:00 in the morning, I do. But you can bet I don't do it very often. And I cannot imagine doing this job without that kind of access or going through the layers, as I said before.

Question: So, this leads naturally enough to a question about relationship with faculty.
Answer: Sure. So I'll tell you one story. It was early in my career at Michigan, when the job I had was the associate VP for state relations. A panel presentation was being made to the faculty on the role of different units of the university. The VP for university relations introduced his three

lieutenants, and we all spoke a bit about what it is that we do, and how we fill our day. Well, sure enough, a faculty member stood up in the question and answer period and said, "I find it offensive that you would claim to speak for me." I looked at him and said, "Why sir, I would never claim to speak for you. I speak for the University of Michigan." And then he sat down.

I hoped what that did was to convey that I had respect for him as an individual, and he could speak for himself, but that my job was not to speak for him. And I keep that in mind, because as you know, there are many times when faculty members are perceived to be doing unbelievably controversial things. I am always interested in trying to shape the views of our stakeholders on what the University of Michigan is doing, and try to help put in context some of the activities or practices that they may find objectionable. But my interactions with faculty for the most part are helped by the fact that I have a faculty advisory committee, a group that meets with me four, five times a year. We break down some of the activities that my office is responsible for. They ask questions. I provide them with insights about all sorts of decisions that we make, or the positions we take. They get an insight into how we approach our work, and I get the benefit of their views and suggestions, so it helps to have that kind of connection.

I have a working relationship with all of the deans. I work with individual faculty members in trying to advance an idea or project or get involved in grant requests, and I turn to faculty when I need a resource to respond to legislators or others for specific expertise. For the most part, it works well. Are there faculty who can be grumpy? Sure. But I think, in general, that we're advancing the institution, and what we must always keep in mind is that the faculty are a very, very important part of the institution. And the way the public understands the institution is not always through the faculty lens. We're frequently in a translational mode on their behalf. And I think some of the most challenging times, frankly, are ones when I'm with faculty who just look at me and ask, "Why don't they understand what we do?"

Question: Do you interact with the board of trustees?
Answer: Extensively! In Michigan, members of our board of regents are

elected. They are nominated by their party and run in statewide elections. Even though I worked for two Republican members of Congress, the transition to a nonpartisan/bipartisan profile at the university was important. I have frequent interactions with the individual board members, and at least right now, we have a few members of the board who have a government relations background as well—so they know the work.

Question: If you had to name one or several characteristics that define your approach to the job, what would they be?

Answer: First, I believe it is essential to be comfortable in an environment that by definition is complex and demanding. In a public institution, almost everything is in the open, and as a result, you have to be able to withstand the shots across the bow and the frontal attacks from the media, from legislators and other stakeholders.

Second, I have come to realize that this work almost always requires being able to negotiate ambiguity. For people who want to see issues and outcomes in black and white, this work can be painful. But if you can negotiate ambiguity, your ability to be satisfied and successful is more likely.

Third, government relations work is not like curing cancer. A healthy dose of humility helps to put the work into perspective. I like to say that I'm a small cog in a very big wheel, and that reminder keeps me pretty well grounded.

And last, I love my work. The pace and the diversity of issues that fill the hours of every single day stimulate me.

CHAPTER ELEVEN

Have a Nice Life

The Government Relations Officer's Career

President Gee's Epiphany

In the summer of 2008, Gordon Gee, newly appointed president of Ohio State University, traveled throughout the state of Ohio to reconnect with Ohioans after eleven years away serving as president of Brown University and Vanderbilt University. Quoted in the August 8, 2008, issue of the *Gongwer Report*, Ohio's Statehouse News Service, Dr. Gee said the trip around the state "confirmed . . . that success in the governmental and public arena is imperative." Nearly a year later, in the spring 2009 issue of *The Presidency*, he wrote that it "underscored the unmatched power of higher education to change lives" (p. 18). Cognizant of the need for universities to do more for their communities, he reorganized his senior leadership team. He created the position of senior vice president for university communications at a salary of $336,000. The person who formerly did communications under the title of senior vice president for university relations was given a new title of senior vice president for government affairs. His salary continued at $324,900.

What can we make of this personnel action and of Dr. Gee's quotes? Arguably, the most experienced and high-profile university president in the country, Gee has always known that politics was important for the survival of higher education. During his first stint as Ohio State University president, he was notorious for wandering through the statehouse in Columbus buttonholing legislators. In his second term at Ohio State, Gee was willing to spend a great deal of money creating equal positions of communications and government affairs.

Ohio State University does not seem to have any serious problems. The largest university in the country, OSU enjoys high popularity. It is flooded with student applications, and has significantly raised its admissions standards. Its research funding has increased dramatically. Its foundation has assets exceeding $2 billion. Its hospital system dominates central Ohio. Its athletic teams have had great success.

So what was important enough to grab Gordon Gee's attention while traveling around Ohio? The answer to this question, at the end of this chapter, is also the conclusion of this book. But before we get to that, let's examine some specific aspects of government relations as a profession in higher education.

Human Resources

Ohio State has a senior vice president for government affairs. Chapter 10 featured interviews with three government relations officers with three distinctly different job titles and responsibilities. Stuart Connock, highlighted at the end of chapter 4, has the title of executive assistant to the president for state governmental relations at the University of Virginia. In general, however, the *top* government relations officer at a university has the title of "vice president of," or "director of," or just "assistant to the president." Staff members are often associates or assistants, as in "associate vice president" or "assistant director." Occasionally, a person will be called a government relations specialist. As is true of Mr. Connock, the word "state" is sometimes inserted in a title to designate specific duties. The term "community" often is used to identify someone who deals with local governments. And, of course, "federal" is used for someone who monitors national political affairs.

Salarywise, a *Chronicle of Higher Education* article entitled "Pay of Senior Administrators Still Beats Inflation, Even in Sluggish Economy" (February 27, 2009, p. A22) pegs the median salary, for all institutions, of the "Chief external-affairs officer" at $150,681. No specific job title using the word "government" appears in the *Chronicle's* "top-level job categories," so external affairs could include government relations, communications, community relations, and/or development. The key to making more than the median pay would be to hold a rank at the vice presidential

level—that is, being part of what is often called the "senior leadership" at
the university—and/or holding dual responsibility, such as vice president
for communications and government relations, or vice president for development and government relations.

The pay for government relations staff members varies widely among
institutions. This is true partly because people in government relations usually do not rise in the ranks as higher education administrators
in the same way as student affairs and finance administrators do. For
example, an older faculty member who begins doing government relations work starts at his faculty salary base, whereas a young person new
to the field but doing the same job would be paid considerably less. The
Chronicle, under a separate "External affairs" category, lists the median
salary of a "Director, federal relations" at $122,037, and the "Director,
state-government relations" at $102,733 (p. A23). In reality, however, a
younger person starting out in government relations can expect to be paid
considerably less.

In higher education, degrees still matter, even in a field that does not
require degrees. A new government relations officer with a doctorate will
earn more than a government relations officer with a bachelor's degree.
Beyond salary, however, an advanced degree is essential in dealing with
faculty members and administrators on campus. This may not be rational,
but it is the truth. Remember that faculty and administrators are hired by
the university to create new knowledge and to conduct research. To faculty,
administrators, and people across campus alike, degrees are well-deserved
symbols of achievement and intellect. Experience may not be as important
as it is in the world outside of higher education. Inside the world of higher
education, a degree matters, and an advanced degree matters more.

The perks for government relations jobs are generally better than for
many other higher education administrative positions. Having access to
the university president usually means having a nicer office in the administration building, near the president and not in a basement cubicle. A
nice office is a necessity because of the need to host politicians and government officials on campus. Some government relations officers have
leased cars or car allowances, although both of these perks are becoming
rarer. On the upside, however, more universities are providing significant
allowances for cell phones and laptops. In addition to having cars, phones,

and a nice office, government relations officers tend to travel extensively. One's state capital may not be the garden spot of the state, but it probably has some good restaurants. And, let's face it, if you are in government relations, you have to love going to Washington.

Pathways

I have made the point a number of times that there are many ways to become a government relations officer at a university. In the three examples from chapter 10, Margie Rolf came from a political family, Rich Lewis wanted a government grant, and Cynthia Wilbanks worked for congressmen. Those three backgrounds are as valid as any other. An English background is as valid as one in political science or chemistry. In fact, my own mentor, who spent almost all of his life in politics before retiring, has a degree in landscape architecture.

A love of the political process—that is, love of government as opposed to party politics—is necessary. Rabid party politicians rarely make good government relations officers. I also contend that the greatest elected officials are *not* rabid party devotees. The public persona for elected officials can be downright nasty toward the opposition, especially during election time, but politicians usually respect and are friendly with many of their counterparts across the aisle. If that were not so, few laws would ever be passed.

Women have excellent opportunities in higher education government relations. In recent years, more women have entered politics, both as elected officials and as administrators in government agencies. Recently, all of Arizona's major state elected officials were women. In Ohio, nine of the nineteen administrators who deal primarily with state government relations for four-year public universities are women. Government relations is an excellent career choice for women hoping to work within the top levels of university administration.

The $50 Donation

Every government relations officer must learn how to deal with requests for donations from politicians. University administrators and faculty members are also asked to donate, of course. There is no single right way to handle these requests, and any decision to make political donations is subject to institutional policies and state ethics rules and regulations. Still, some general guidelines apply for most government relations officers.

If you work at a public institution, do not make a deal with the president or vice president that you will use any extra income afforded to make equivalent donations to politicians and political parties. This is ethically wrong and probably illegal, in most, if not all, states. It is also unnecessary. Politicians long ago realized that university employees, from presidents to faculty members to staff members (even if they belong to unions), do not make significant political donations. It is just a fact of political life.

On the other hand, there is no restriction against a government relations officer's making personal contributions to politicians and campaigns. Just don't naively assume that your name will not be duly noted by candidates from the opposing political party. The Republicans will notice if you give only to Democrats, and vice versa. Being self-righteous about this topic ("I'll give as much as I want, to whomever I want!") means that you will probably have a short career as a government relations officer.

Seldom, if ever, pay the published price to attend political fund-raisers. Most fund-raisers start at $250 and go up and up from there. But there is nothing wrong with saying that you can afford to pay only $50, or even $100. Politicians will be happy to take a check, and even happier if university representatives attend the fund-raiser. But be careful about promising to bring top university officials with you to a fund-raiser without first knowing that they are able and willing to attend. It is also okay if a president occasionally makes an appearance. Be certain, though, that she knows to bring a personal check and not a university check. Incidentally, understand that in most states a politician's professional staff is not allowed, by law or rule, to participate in fund-raising and campaigns. A whole different set of people raise money and run campaigns. Never put professional staff in an awkward position by asking about a fund-raiser, or by giving them a check to pass on.

Finally, for Pete's sake, do not try to attend every event. No one expects you to do that. Stay away from fund-raisers sponsored by two or more politicians, or by partisan political groups like the Democratic House Caucus, and say no to golf tournaments (they are expensive, and you may not even see the host). Remember, the purpose of going to any fund-raiser is to get some face time with the politician (in this venue, he is obliged to be nice to you) and to meet a few other influential people.

On Campus/Off Campus

One of the greatest challenges faced by a university government relations officer, one not faced by most other lobbyists, is balancing a visible presence on campus while seeing to many off-campus duties. More than most other institutions and businesses, universities define themselves in part by their campus setting. A place of beauty and intellect, a campus is both the physical grounds of a university, college, or school and the very idea of community.

In this era of computers, e-mail, and iPhones, a person can be in touch with anyone, anywhere the world, from an on-campus office. The federal government and the states broadcast, via television and the computer, most legislative proceedings as well as important government and agency announcements. Even local-access telecommunications will bring you city and county government proceedings. In fact, because of the expense of travel and the time involved, many government relations officers do spend more of their time on campus. Being on campus facilitates an important aspect of the government relations officer's job, one that is often ignored: a government relations officer must spend some time net-working with key individuals within the university. Because he or she has direct access to the president and other members of the senior leadership team, a government relations officer may come to believe that becoming acquainted with other members of the university community is not all that necessary. But apart from the university's president, provost, and senior officers, it is important that a government relations officer knows—by both name and sight—the following key individuals:

- student government officers
- editorial staff of the student newspaper
- most of the communications staff who deal with the media
- members of the facilities staff, especially those involved in construct-ing buildings

- officers of any labor unions on campus
- the most prominent researchers, especially those who have received direct earmarks from the federal government or the state
- the administrator in charge of the agenda and of communicating with the institution's trustees

Nevertheless, a government relations officer must spend considerable time off campus. Politicians, government agency officials, and (if applicable) university system administrators must personally know the main university contact for government matters. Further, a government relations officer must get to know the administrative assistants and support staff for politicians and various others. These are the people who act as gatekeepers and who know what legislation is being considered. And, more than most other university administrators, government relations officers depend on contact with and information from their peers at other universities. University government relations officers are usually a tight-knit group, and go out of their way to support one another.

It is a constant balancing act (or magic act) for government relations officers to be in two places at once—both on and off campus. Here are a couple of suggestions (or tricks) to help. In chapter 10, Cynthia Wilbanks describes creating a faculty advisory committee that meets regularly. Such committees can ensure that the government relations officer appears engaged in campus issues. Advisory committees also help solidify working relationships with key campus constituents. Regular e-mail newsletters are another way that campus personnel and politicians can be kept up-to-date on government relations activities and priorities, as well as off-campus university publicity. In a similar vein, an interview in the student newspaper or other campus publication is a great way for the government relations officer to maintain visibility at home. After all, government relations officers (almost) always have something interesting to talk about.

The Governing Board

Throughout this book, I have mentioned how a university's board of trustees or a state's board of regents affects government relations. Oversight civilian boards vary widely in terms of size, power, and influence, yet they are almost always made up of members who are more politically active and politically connected than the average person. This means that board members often are interested in the functioning of the university's government relations officer. Just as some board members are particularly interested in the university's finances and others are particularly interested in athletics, there are always at least two or three board members who are vitally interested in what the university is doing in the world of politics.

Of course, it is primarily the university's president who must deal with these politically active board members. The president also has an obligation to protect his government relations staff, because board members are generally partisan and also (sometimes unwittingly) make inappropriate political requests. The president cannot allow a board member to interfere with the work of a government relations officer, but it happens sometimes. A phone call is made to buy tickets for a political fund-raiser. The son of a political crony wants to be admitted to the university or, worse still, wants a job. A politician asks a board member for a block of tickets for the next home football game. The requests are endless. Some board members, who seldom, if ever, get paid for putting in many hours of work, figure that doing a small political favor is the least the university can do.

But political favors are not possible, and any government relations officer who receives an inappropriate request must document and report the request immediately to his direct supervisor and/or president. This can become a very uncomfortable situation. Still, no matter how uncomfortable it might be at the moment, dealing with the issue is far preferable to reading in the newspapers about the university's administration granting inappropriate favors to politicians.

Asking a board member to speak to a politician about a government issue is acceptable. Of course, the request must be both ethical and legal, but it is perfectly reasonable, for example, for a board member to write a letter to the chair of the state senate's finance committee to request a boost in funding for the university. A call to a congressperson to endorse a university earmark is also acceptable. The one proviso here is that the board member tell the university president what she is doing.

The Future as a Consultant

For some of us, university government relations is a career. But it is not for everyone. Universities pay good salaries and have excellent benefits, and it is hard to give those up. Still, normal pathways of career advancement in the university structure are limited, particularly if the government relations officer does not have an advanced degree. The only two university areas that may be attractive for government relations officers are the university's communications/public relations office and the development office. Both of these offices work primarily with constituents who are beyond the perimeter of the campus, which therefore should be in the comfort zone of government relations officers. Like government relations, careers in development and public relations require staff members to be well-dressed. It would be a shame for government relations people not to be able to use all those expensive clothes in their next job.

Another suitable post-government relations career is government consulting. Such consulting can be done through a private lobbying firm or with an association related to higher education or industry. These jobs are available both for young professionals and for veteran government relations officers, but they usually involve relocating to the state capital or Washington, or to some "think tank" center, which may not be possible or convenient. Nevertheless, these are options, and the pay is similar to if not better than salaries at a university. One thing to keep in mind is that consulting requires a person to be an effective salesman. Consultants/lobbyists must pitch themselves and their services, and cannot take it personally when they are turned down, which happens often.

An alternative to joining a lobbying firm or association is to work as an independent consultant. This is especially attractive for retirees with a pension, or for someone who has a spouse with an income. Starting one's own business—whether it is consulting or some other enterprise—is difficult at best. But the rewards of working when and where you want, and working on projects that interest you, are great. Though the field of "political consulting" always seems crowded during elections, in reality there are not that many people who have the background and contacts to pursue it successfully. Working for some years in university government relations should provide both the background and the contacts for one to be successful.

What President Gee Found While Traveling through Ohio

What President Gee found was what he would have found if he had been traveling throughout West Virginia, Colorado, Rhode Island, or Tennessee, the home states of the other universities where he has been president. He found that higher education has fallen in terms of reputation and importance among Americans. Still considered a necessity of life, higher education is now perceived by students as an expensive and grueling four-year effort to get a halfway decent job. Parents speak of sacrificing to send their kids to college. Students complain of having to hold down a couple of jobs while taking a full load of classes. All of higher education seems to the general populace to be out of touch with what is really needed if the nation is to succeed in today's world, especially during the recent economic downturn.

Legislators at the state and federal levels across the country continue to receive and respond to complaints about higher education from their constituents. Institutions have different and confusing admission standards. Financial aid forms are impossible to fill out. Credits will not transfer between state schools. Tuition keeps going up. Room and board costs keep rising. Professors do not always do a good job of teaching. Foreign graduate students and faculty who lack decent English-speaking skills are teaching classes. Textbooks are too expensive. Classrooms and laboratories are shabby and run-down. University bureaucracies are not responsive to questions or problems. Businesses complain that newly hired graduates are not well prepared for the workplace. The list of perceived university failings seems endless.

Many of these complaints have been heard for years. But what has higher education done to respond? Practically nothing, except to go after more funding from state legislatures and research sources while continuing to increase tuition. Higher education asserts, with much merit, that its financial needs are great. But state legislatures in general have been parsimonious. They have cut university subsidies year after year while knowing full well that universities must then raise student tuition to make up for the cuts. Universities have been faced with increasing costs for the utilities, services, and supplies needed to keep campuses functioning. And across the country, aging campus buildings are falling apart while legislators, students, and governing boards are demanding that universities construct new science labs and wire their campuses with the latest in computer technology.

Meanwhile, during all this internal strife and a push-me-pull-me relationship with state government, other sectors of society have increasingly looked at campuses—both public and private—and have wondered why their vast array of resources are not used beyond traditional college classroom teaching. For example, K-12 school systems want universities to provide more on-the-job teacher training, and to offer opportunities for high school students to take college-level courses. Neighborhoods want universities to provide jobs for residents, and to patrol the local streets using university police. Municipalities want universities to provide leadership and technical expertise for economic development. Universities have been surprised by such unsolicited requests, many of which require large sums of money.

Even small institutions of higher education have relatively large payrolls and foundations, as well as endowments in the millions. Local governments want universities to share the cost of infrastructure improvements. Local entrepreneurs want free advice and support. Local charities want donations. Local social agencies want volunteers and funding. The list of requests never ends.

Beyond pleas for help and money, there are more meaningful requests. These have far-reaching consequences, and are the basis for the restructuring of universities as we know them. Quoting President Trani again, "In recent years, it has become increasingly apparent that more communities and regions, in the United States and abroad, are coming to believe that developing stronger partnerships with their local universities is crucial to the capacity to flourish and provide their citizens with a worthwhile life." *A worthwhile life!* That implies that a worthwhile life is not to be achieved by a young person simply by putting in four years of classroom and library study and then graduating with a diploma. That means that a worthwhile life is being defined differently in today's society than it was in yesterday's society. Even if yesterday was just last week.

Like it or not, higher education today is defined in terms of economics. Whether it is the state providing subsidy, or the federal government granting research funding, or parents and students paying tuition, everyone wants a return on investment, or ROI. This notion, ROI, appears over and over again in the burgeoning literature equating higher education with the economy. ROI for governments, parents, and students means that students graduate with skills that are translatable into employment (with a preference for high-tech employment), and all this should be possible without running up excessive debt. Students might then become motivated to stay within the states in which they are citizens and/or graduated. Increasingly, the goals of higher education today are to prepare students to enter the workforce, to foster the creation of business and industry for those students to work in, and to see the local and state economies grow.

Of course, these goals are anathema to the long-established traditions and missions of most institutions of higher education. I use the word "most" here because online universities such as the University of Phoenix have expanded on the premise of giving students a practical education at a lower cost. (In reality, the cost actually is not that much lower, but the *impression* people have is that it is much lower.) Still, universities face roadblocks to change, oftentimes from their own faculties.

The problem is that faculty and many administrators are taking personally this transition to a more socially involved and politically connected university. This is not about the English professor who is willing to fight to the death to protect his course on Thoreau. (I know, how ironic.) What the professor does not realize is that even the most fervent anti-university state legislator is not interested in removing Thoreau from the curriculum. Only a few fringe legislators want to tell teachers what to teach, and most of these are only hung up on creationism. What the vast majority of legislators (and the citizens who elect them and pay to send their children to school) really want is for universities to demonstrate in practical ways that students are receiving a good education, one that will help them become well-rounded and employable citizens.

This is the worthwhile life—one that includes reading Henry David Thoreau but also being able to write a coherent paragraph about Thoreau's work and being able to add up the tables of expenses that Thoreau kept in his journal. University faculties have a huge opportunity at this moment in time to redefine curricula, and to reassess what a graduate of an American university thinks about, talks about, and does. This opportunity, however, is slipping away, both as government officials decide to monitor higher education more closely while demanding affordability and accountability, and as senior administrators increasingly realize that the very existence of their institutions resides not in defending the past but in embracing the future.

This, then, is the point where the role of the university government relations officer becomes critical to higher education. An office of government relations is often the *only* administrative bridge to the various levels of government that profoundly affect universities. It is also yet another sign of the apocalypse. Presidents of private universities—especially the smaller private universities—have no recourse or support to draw upon in coping with the perilous and changing winds of government. Meanwhile, the larger state universities—bolstered by their federal research components and the diversity of their students and degrees—as well as professional schools are the institutions best able to respond to government, and to participate in multi-level government initiatives such as economic development.

It may seem odd that when OSU President Gee completed his Ohio tour, he created a new communications administrator position with a salary of $300,000 a year. Another administrator, with the sole job of coordinating government relations, received the same salary. Gee understands that legislators hate the proclivity of universities to employ high-paid administrators. Gee also knows, however, that as the president of the largest university in the nation, he must communicate the university's efforts to bolster the economy of the state, and must also coordinate the government relations efforts with support for the university's advancement of economic development. This is not unique to Ohio State. It is also what Vice President for Government Relations Cynthia Wilbanks is doing at the University of Michigan. It is what the truly progressive major universities of the country have realized needs to be done. But it is also what all of us must do. In the front ranks of this effort for institutional success, is the government relations officer. That is the career. That is the mission.

BIBLIOGRAPHY

Altbach, Philip G., Robert O. Berdahl, and Patricia J. Gumport, eds. 2005. *American Higher Education in the Twenty-First Century: Social, Political, and Economic Challenges*, 2nd ed. Baltimore: The Johns Hopkins University Press.

Bloland, Harland G. 1985. *Associations in Action: The Washington, D.C., Higher Education Community*. Washington: The Association for the Study of Higher Education.

Brint, Steven, ed. 2002. *The Future of the City of Intellect: The Changing American University*. Stanford: Stanford University Press.

Cook, Constance Ewing. 1998. *Lobbying for Higher Education: How Colleges and Universities Influence Federal Policies*. Nashville: Vanderbilt University Press.

Fischer, Karin. 2008. "Struggling Communities Turn to Colleges." *Chronicle of Higher Education*, May 16, pp. 1, 17–20.

Friedman, Thomas L. 2005. *The World is Flat*. New York: Farrar, Straus, and Giroux.

Glenn, David. 2009. "The Power of Everyday Life: Political Scientists, Taking Their Cue from Anthropologists, Try Fieldwork." *Chronicle of Higher Education*, September 21, pp. B13–14.

Guess, Andy. 2008. "Fish to Prof: Stick to Teaching." *Inside Higher Ed*, July 1 (online).

Kerr, Clark. 2002. "Shock Wave II: An Introduction to the Twenty-First Century," pp. 15–16. In Brint, Steven, ed. *The Future of the City of Intellect: The Changing American University*. Stanford, Calif.: Stanford University Press.

Lieberman, Joseph I. 2000. *In Praise of Public Life*. New York: Simon & Schuster.

Mack, Charles S. 1997. *Business, Politics, and the Practice of Government Relations*. Westport, Connecticut: Quorum Books.

Mariani, Mack D., and Gordon J. Hewitt. 2008. "Indoctrination U.? Faculty Ideology and Changes in Student Political Orientation." *PS: Political Science & Politics*. Vol. 41, issue 4, October, pp. 773–83. Published online by Cambridge University Press, 1 Oct. 2008.

Maurrasse, David. 2001. *Beyond the Campus: How Colleges and Universities Form Partnerships with their Communities*. New York: Routledge.

Millett, John D. 1974. *Politics and Higher Education*. Tuscaloosa: The University of Alabama Press.

Obey, David R. 2007. *Raising Hell for Justice: The Washington Battles of a Heartland Progressive*. Madison: The University of Wisconsin Press.

Phelan, Adele. 2009. "What 'Entrepreneurship' Entails." *Trusteeship*, January/February, p. 37.

Reid, Irvin D. 2008. "The Urban University: Catalyst for Renewal." *The Presidency*, fall, pp. 30–34.

Rhodes, Frank H.T. 2001. *The Creation of the Future: The Role of the American University*. Ithaca: N.Y.: Cornell University Press.

Rosenzweig, Robert M. 1998. *The Political University: Policy, Politics, and Presidential Leadership in the American Research University*. Baltimore: The Johns Hopkins University Press.

Townsend, Barbara K., and Susan B. Twombly, eds. 2000. *Community Colleges: Policy in the Future Context*. Westport, Conn.: ABLEX Publishing.

Trachtenberg, Stephen Joel. 2008. *Big Man on Campus: A University President Speaks Out on Higher Education*. New York: Simon & Schuster.

Trani, Eugene P. 2008. "Even in Hard Times, Colleges Should Help Their Communities." *Chronicle of Higher Education*, May 16, p. 36.

Wills, Garry. 1994. *Certain Trumpets: The Call of Leaders*. New York: Simon & Schuster.

Zemsky, Robert, Gregory R. Wegner and William F. Massy. 2006. *Remaking the American University: Market-Smart and Mission-Centered*. New Brunswick, N.J.: Rutgers University Press.

INDEX